A Pyth
Guide for Web
Scraping

*Explore Python Tools, Web Scraping
Techniques, and How to Automata
Data for Industrial Applications*

Pradumna Milind Panditrao

www.bpbonline.com

FIRST EDITION 2021

Copyright © BPB Publications, India

ISBN: 978-93-90684-991

Distributors:

BPB PUBLICATIONS
20, Ansari Road, Darya Ganj
New Delhi-110002
Ph: 23254990/23254991

DECCAN AGENCIES
4-3-329, Bank Street,
Hyderabad-500195
Ph: 24756967/24756400

MICRO MEDIA
Shop No. 5, Mahendra Chambers,
150 DN Rd. Next to Capital Cinema,
V.T. (C.S.T.) Station, MUMBAI-400 001
Ph: 22078296/22078297

BPB BOOK CENTRE
376 Old Lajpat Rai Market,
Delhi-110006
Ph: 23861747

To View Complete
BPB Publications Catalogue
Scan the QR Code:

Published by Manish Jain for BPB Publications, 20 Ansari Road, Darya Ganj, New Delhi-110002 and Printed by him at Repro India Ltd, Mumbai

www.bpbonline.com

Dedicated to

My beloved Parents:
Shri Milind Panditrao, Smita Panditrao
&
My wife Suchitra and My Daughter Rajvika

About the Author

I am **Pradumna Panditrao**. I have done Masters in Networking & Telecommunication. I have a total of 8+ years of experience in various domains like Software Development, DevOps Automation tools, Data mining Crawling tools, Cloud Technologies, Hardware Profiling. I have published a paper on Cognitive Radio, 4G Technology Algorithms. Currently working as Sr. Software Engineer as DevOps tool Developer. I have given Embedded software development Lectures and Lab demo sessions at BitsPilani Goa in 2014-2015

About the Reviewer

Vibhu Bansal is an entrepreneur and founder of ITSYS Solutions. He has about 22 years' experience in software development. From an early age, he had an interest in data and analytics and worked on numerous MIS applications for private sector and government organizations in India. Under him, ITSYS Solutions his been providing web scraping services since 2007 to businesses in North America & Europe.

Acknowledgement

There are a few people I want to thank for the continued and ongoing support they have given me during the writing of this book. First and foremost, I would like to thank my parents for continuously encouraging me for writing the book — I could have never completed this book without their support.

I am grateful to the course and the companies which gave me support throughout the learning process of web scraping and very important to learn the tools related to web scraping.

Thank you for the all hidden support provided. I gratefully acknowledged Mr. Vibhu Bansal for his kind technical scrutiny for this book.

My gratitude also goes to the team at BPB Publications for being supportive enough to provide me quite a long time to finish the first part of the book and also allow me to publish the book in multiple parts, since image processing, being a vast and very active area of research, it was impossible to deep-dive into different class of problems in a single book, especially by not making it too voluminous.

Preface

This book covers many different aspects of web scraping, the importance of automation of web scraping. This book also introduces the importance of web scraping in the field of real time industry. It shows how the data is important for the industries. This book solves the basic understanding towards web scraping / crawling in the data world. It also gives importance for python learning. So that python's basic concepts get refreshed. This book gives information about the usefulness of Python in web scraping as well.

This book takes a practical approach for web scraping learners. It covers few realtime industry examples as well. It will cover information such as Python Basically used for automation, machine learning. It can be used for easy data manipulating and transforming. Used in different domains for data mining purposes. You can design API access frameworks for end to end automation in different domains like finance, retails etc.

This book is divided into 10 chapters. They will cover Python basics, basics and advance in web scraping, why python is better for web scraping, real time example in web scraping etc. So learners can get more interest in web scraping tools as well.The details are listed below.

Chapter 1 will learn what is Python, Why python is a better language apart from other Programming languages. In Python Basics, covers the key features of python. Will explain about how python is easy to learn. Will explain about the internals for Python. Will explain about different modules, packages in Python. I will give some more information about python's Capability of object-oriented, high level programming Language. Will explain about the debugging capability of Python, and how it is more convenient. Python is an interpreter language and there are extensive standard libraries available. Will explain about the memory structure of

Python. Differnece in Python version 2.x vs 3.x. Will give details about Installation of Python on different Operating Systems.

Chapter 2 will cover Python Use cases, will explain in the case. Give basic details about Python syntax. When to use and what to use in case of different varieties of examples.

Chapter 3 will cover As Python is Object-oriented Language, we can use it as per requirement. We can create the different functions, classes as per the requirement. Python is also used for test automation. It can be used for test automation and design framework for test automation.

Chapter 4 will cover information such as Python Basically used for automation, machine learning. It can be used for easy data manipulating and transforming. Used in different domains for data mining purposes. You can design API access frameworks for end to end automation in different domains like finance, retails etc.

Chapter 5 Web Scraping, Basically web scraping is used for extracting data from different sites. There are many parts of web scraping such as web mining, data mining, web indexing. So collected data can be shown in the format of convenient users.

Chapter 6 will cover information as , Industries need data for different types of analysis from the web. So In that scenario web scraping is very useful

Chapter 7 explains, Python is one of the Programming languages. Everyone thinks of why python only for web scraping.

- Large no. of Libraries
- Easy to use
- Dynamically type
- Good community for solutions
- Syntax is much easier.

Chapter 8 is to explain how to get fun inside the web scraping automation will help. Automation will be helpful for scraping and solving real world problems. So there is a big role of web scraping in data mining as well with different automation tools.

Chapter 9 explains, Web scraping is getting used for different and important parts of business nowadays.

Chapter 10 explains There are lots of benefits to use web scraping in day to day life for Industries.

Downloading the coloured images:

Please follow the link to download the
Coloured Images of the book:

https://rebrand.ly/6c7632r

Errata

We take immense pride in our work at BPB Publications and follow best practices to ensure the accuracy of our content to provide with an indulging reading experience to our subscribers. Our readers are our mirrors, and we use their inputs to reflect and improve upon human errors, if any, that may have occurred during the publishing processes involved. To let us maintain the quality and help us reach out to any readers who might be having difficulties due to any unforeseen errors, please write to us at :

errata@bpbonline.com

Your support, suggestions and feedbacks are highly appreciated by the BPB Publications' Family.

Did you know that BPB offers eBook versions of every book published, with PDF and ePub files available? You can upgrade to the eBook version at www.bpbonline.com and as a print book customer, you are entitled to a discount on the eBook copy. Get in touch with us at :

business@bpbonline.com for more details.

At **www.bpbonline.com**, you can also read a collection of free technical articles, sign up for a range of free newsletters, and receive exclusive discounts and offers on BPB books and eBooks.

BPB is searching for authors like you

If you're interested in becoming an author for BPB, please visit **www.bpbonline.com** and apply today. We have worked with thousands of developers and tech professionals, just like you, to help them share their insight with the global tech community. You can make a general application, apply for a specific hot topic that we are recruiting an author for, or submit your own idea.

The code bundle for the book is also hosted on GitHub at **https://github.com/bpbpublications/A-Python-Guide-for-Web-Scraping**. In case there's an update to the code, it will be updated on the existing GitHub repository.

We also have other code bundles from our rich catalog of books and videos available at **https://github.com/bpbpublications**. Check them out!

PIRACY

If you come across any illegal copies of our works in any form on the internet, we would be grateful if you would provide us with the location address or website name. Please contact us at :

business@bpbonline.com with a link to the material.

If you are interested in becoming an author

If there is a topic that you have expertise in, and you are interested in either writing or contributing to a book, please visit **www.bpbonline.com**.

REVIEWS

Please leave a review. Once you have read and used this book, why not leave a review on the site that you purchased it from? Potential readers can then see and use your unbiased opinion to make purchase decisions, we at BPB can understand what you think about our products, and our authors can see your feedback on their book. Thank you!

For more information about BPB, please visit **www.bpbonline.com**.

Table of Contents

CHAPTER 1
Python Basics

1.1 Introduction

Python is one of the most famous programming languages in software development. Python is an interpreted, high-level, general-purpose programming language. It is a general-purpose coding language—which means that unlike HTML, CSS, and JavaScript, it can be used for programming and software development in addition to web development.

1.2 Structure

In this chapter we will discuss the following topics:

- History of Python
- Basics of Python
- Python internals
- Installing Python on different operating systems
- Different aspects of Python
- Capabilities of Python

1.3 Objective

After studying this chapter, you should be able to:

- Understand the Python history
- Install Python on different operating systems
- Understand Python from different aspects and its capabilities

1.4 Python and its history

Python is a general-purpose, high-level, interpreted, object-oriented open source programming language. Python was designed in the 1980s by *Guido van Rossum* as a side project and later implemented by the **Python Software Foundation** (**PSF**). Python was finally released in 1991. It was designed to reduce the large code size of C, JAVA, and C++, in turn improving time efficiency and productivity of developers.

Nowadays Python is famous for different reasons. Python has compatibility benefits with different versions of it. Python can be used for different purposes such as web development (GUI applications, websites), system-level programming, machine-level programming, developing IoT applications, etc. As Python is highly abstracted from the assembly language, it can be used to provide instructions to the CPU. It is helpful for rapid application programming as it has a high-level build in data structures. Python offers fast development cycle with test cycle speeds as it is not affected by segmentation fault errors, making debugging very easy. As it is an interpreted language, in case of errors, it returns an exception. When the program doesn't catch the exception, the interpreter prints a stack trace.

1.4.1 Python versions

Python 3.7.x and 3.9.0 are the latest versions. The two most widely used versions of Python are Python 2.x and 3.x. There is a lot of competition between the two and both of them seem to have quite a number of different supporters. As of January 1, 2020, the 2.x branch of the Python programming language is no longer supported by its developers, the Python Software Foundation.

Python is used for various purposes such as developing, scripting, generation, and software testing. Due to its beauty for programming and simplicity, top organizations like, Google, Quora, Mozilla,

Hewlett-Packard, Qualcomm, IBM, and Cisco have implemented Python for development.

Figure 1.1: *Python version Cycle*

1.5 Preference of Python over others

Following are the reasons for choosing Python as your programming language:

- **Open-source framework**: Basically, the Python language is open-source, so we can use several open-source Python frameworks, libraries, and development tools to reduce development time and operating costs. Programming is easy with an IDE.

- **Useful and robust libraries**: Python offers a large collection of useful libraries which can support all possible use cases of a developer. Different modules can be used by developers to meet their specific needs.

- **Compatibility with different platforms and systems**: Python is supported on multiple operating systems like OSx, Windows, Linux, etc. You can build Python on specific versions, get dependencies, and make compatible versions. For example, you can create a Python program on CentOS 4.5 and run it on a later version of the operating system.

- **Supports prototype-based programming**: It supports different prototypes like object-orientation support. It supports automatic memory management and multithreaded programming. This feature is useful for designing very complex applications with a variety of features.

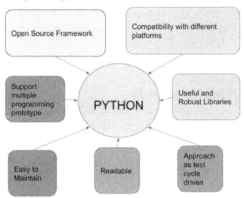

Figure 1.2: Python usability

- **Easy to maintain**: Maintenance of application and reusability of code are the top-most priorities of any programmer. Python definitely fits in these criteria as it supports virtual environments (we will cover virtual environments later in the chapter). It means that you can change the version of Python as per the requirement of your application.

- **Readable**: Python code has high-readability. We can customize a Python application without adding much code due its clean code base.

- **Test cycle driven**: As application development is rapid with Python, its testing cycle is also fast. Python can be used to design APIs based on a test cycle framework.

1.6 Python internals

To learn more about the Python framework, let's take a look at *figure 1.3*:

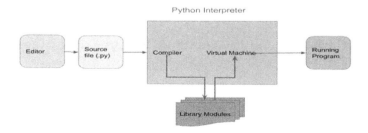

Figure 1.3: Python Internal diagram

The following steps are involved in writing a simple Python program:

1. Write code in the editor.

2. Save the file with a **.py** extension.

3. Compile the code. In this step, the compiler checks the syntax and reports errors, if any. Mainly indentation errors are highlighted.

4. If there are no errors, then the interpreter translates the program into an equivalent intermediate byte code.

5. Byte code is sent to the Python virtual machine. If there are no errors, the program will run successfully.

1.7 Python installation on different operating systems

Python can be installed on different operating systems. You can choose from different installation packages depending on your OS. Basically, following are the prerequisites for installing Python:

- Operating system details such as Mac, Linux, or Windows

- Operating system type whether it is 32-bit or 64 bit

- Python version to be installed

- Methods to get Python interpreter from the official website

- Verifying Python installation

- Running Python code – Script mode or shell mode

- Tools to develop Python code

- Installing modules and third-party libraries. (With help of pip)

1.7.1 On MacOS

Here is the standard process for installing Python on OSx. Follow these steps to install Homebrew on MacOS:

1. Open Terminal or your favorite OS X terminal emulator and run the following command:

```
$    ruby    -e    "$(curl-fsSL    https://raw.
githubusercontent.com/Homebrew/install/master/
install )"
```

The script will explain what changes it will make and prompt you before the installation begins.

2. Once you've installed Homebrew, insert the **Homebrew** directory at the top of your **PATH** environment variable. You can do this by adding the following line at the bottom of your **~/.profile** file:

```
export      PATH="/usr/local/opt/python/libexec/
bin:$PATH"
```

If you have OS X 10.12 (Sierra) or older use this line instead:

```
export PATH=/usr/local/bin:/usr/local/sbin:$PATH
```

3. Now, we can install Python 2.7:

```
$ brew install python@2
```

Because **python@2** is a "**keg**", we need to update our **PATH** again, to point at our new installation:

```
export      PATH="/usr/local/opt/python@2/libexec/
bin:$PATH"
```

Homebrew names the executable **python2** so that you can still run the system Python via the executable Python:

```
export PATH=/usr/local/bin:/usr/local/sbin:$PATH
```

4. Now, we can install Python 3:

```
$ brew install python
```

This will take a minute or two. Homebrew installs pip which pointing to Python3. Do I have a Python 3 installed?

```
$ python -version
```

```
Python 3.7.1 # Success!
```

1.7.2 On Linux

On Debian:

Step 1 – Prerequisites

Use the following command to install prerequisites for Python before installing it:

```
sudo apt-get install build-essential checkinstall
sudo apt-get install libreadline-gplv2-dev libncursesw5-dev libssl-dev \
libsqlite3-dev tk-dev libgdbm-dev libc6-dev libbz2-dev libffi-dev zlib1g-dev
```

Step 2 – Downloading Python 3.7

Download Python using the following command from the official Python website. You can download the latest version instead of the version specified as follows:

```
cd /usr/src
sudo    wget    https://www.python.org/ftp/python/3.7.4/Python-3.7.4.tgz
```

Now extract the downloaded package:

```
sudo tar xzf Python-3.7.4.tgz
```

Step 3 – Compiling the Python source code

Use the following set of commands to compile Python source code on your system using **altinstall**:

```
cd Python-3.7.4
sudo ./configure --enable-optimizations
sudo make altinstall
```

make altinstall is used to prevent replacing the default python binary file /usr/bin/python.

Step 4 – Check Python Version

Check the latest version of Python installed using the following command:

```
python3.7 -V

Python-3.7.4
```

On CentOS:

Following are the steps for installing Python on CentOS:

```
# yum -y groupinstall development
```

```
# yum -y install zlib-devel
```

In Debian we will need to install **gcc**, **make**, and the **zlib** compression/decompression libraries:

```
# aptitude -y install gcc make zlib1g-dev
```

To install Python 3.6, run the following commands:

```
# wget https://www.python.org/ftp/python/3.6.3/Python-3.6.3.tar.xz
```

```
# tar xJf Python-3.6.3.tar.xz
```

```
# cd Python-3.6.3
```

```
# ./configure
```

```
# make
```

```
# make install
```

Now relax and go grab a sandwich because this may take a while. When the installation is complete, use **which** to verify the location of the main binary:

```
# which python3
```

```
# python3 -V
```

1.7.3 On Windows

1. Click on the **Download Windows x86-64** executable installer link under the top-left stable releases from the following link: **https://www.python.org/downloads/**

   Pop-up window titled Opening **python-3.74-amd64.exe** will appear.

2. Click the **Save File** button. The file named **python-3.7.4-amd64.exe** should start downloading to your default download location. This file is about 30 MB in size, so it might

take a while to download y if you are on a slow internet connection.

The file should appear as **python-3.7.4-amd64.exe**.

3. Move this file to a more permanent location, so that you can install Python (and reinstall it later, if necessary).

4. Start the installation by double clicking the file.

5. Navigate to the directory **C:\Users\$USER\AppData\Local\Programs\Python\Python37** (or to the directory where Python was installed: see the pop-up window for installing step 3).

6. Double-click the icon/file **python.exe**.

The following pop-up window will appear:

Figure 1.4: *Python Console on Windows*

In this way we can install Python on different operating systems.

1.7.4 Installing libraries/modules in Python

There are different ways to install modules in Python depending on your operating system. It means that the instructions to install modules in Python may vary depending on your operating system. In the following sections we will learn how to install pip and modules on different operating systems.

1.7.5 Mac and Linux instructions to install pip

On Mac and Linux, we have to download the **get-pip.py** Python file by executing the following command:

```
curl -O https://bootstrap.pypa.io/get-pip.py
```

After the file is downloaded, we can run the file with the help of **sudo** user as:

```
sudo python get-pip.py
```

After this file is executed, **pip** module gets installed. This is later used to install further modules and libraries.

1.7.6 Windows instructions to install pip

The easiest way to install pip on Windows is through the use of a Python program called get-pip.py, which you can download at **https://bootstrap.pypa.io/get-pip.py**.

Once you have saved this file, you need to run it in one of the following ways. If you prefer using a Python interpreter, right-click on the file **get-pip.py** and choose "**open with**" and then choose the Python interpreter of your choice.

If you prefer to install pip using the Windows command line tool, navigate to the directory where you have placed the **get-pip.py** file. For this example, we'll assume this directory is **python27**, so we'll use the command **C:\>cd python27**. Once you are in this directory, run the command:

```
python get-pip.py
```

1.7.7 Installing Python modules

Now that you have pip, it is easy to install Python modules since it does all the work for you. When you find a module that you want to use, the documentation or installation instructions for the module will usually include the necessary **pip** command. For example:

```
sudo pip install requests
sudo pip install beautifulsoup4
sudo pip install simplekml
```

Sometimes, especially on Windows, you may find it helpful to use the **-m** flag option (to help Python find the **pip** module):

```
python -m pip install XXX
```

In this way we can install modules on different operating systems and later import these modules/libraries to get functions workable in the suitable code.

1.8 Virtual environment

A virtual environment basically helps to keep your projects isolated. This kind of need arises when you are working on multiple projects running different versions of Python.

It will create a project-wise structure in the folder and keep Python and pip executable files inside the virtual environment folder.

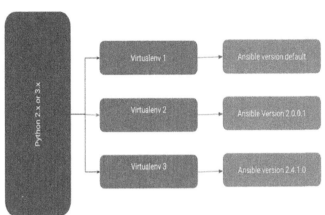

Figure 1.5: *Architecture of virtual environment*

1.8.1 Steps for setting up a virtual environment on Linux

Install virtualenv using pip3:

```
sudo pip3 install virtualenv
```

Now create a virtual environment:

```
virtualenv demo
```

You can use any name instead of **venv**. You can also use a Python interpreter of your choice:

```
virtualenv -p /usr/bin/python2.7 demo
```

Next, we will activate the virtual environment:

```
source demo/bin/activate
```

Using fish shell:

```
source demo/bin/activate.fish
```

To deactivate:

```
Deactivate
```

Create virtualenv using Python3:

```
virtualenv -p python3 myenv
```

Instead of using **virtualenv** you can use this command in Python 3:

```
python3 -m venv demo
```

1.8.2 Setup steps for virtual environment on Windows

Start **virtualenv** and head to your project location in the Windows Command Prompt:

```
pip install virtualenv
```

Once inside the project folder, run the following command:

```
virtualenv env
```

Activate **virtualenv**. On Windows, virtualenv (**venv**) creates a batch file called:

```
\env\Scripts\activate.bat
```

To activate **virtualenv** on Windows, we will activate the script in the Scripts folder:

```
\path\env\Scripts\activate
```

Example:

```
C:\Users\'Username'\venv\Scripts\activate.bat
```

1.9 Editors for Python

As per the usage of Python like developing, scripting, generation, and software testing, we can use editors. There are a variety of editors with different use cases. Mostly I would recommend the following editors:

- Atom (Development)
- Python for Visual Studio (Development)
- Spyder
- PyCharm (Testing)

We can use text editors as well for scripting using Python:

- Notepad ++

For the most part of this book, we will use the VS code editor and the simple text editor as well as the console for Python programming.

1.9.1 Python environment variables

	Variable	Description
1	PYTHONPATH	This describes the python interpreter where to locate module files imported in program
2	PYTHONSTARTUP	Contains Path of initializing python source code. It named as .pythonrc.py in Unix
3	PYTHONCASEOK	In windows to find first case-insensitive match
4	PYTHONHOME	It is alternate to PYTHONPATH module

Table 1.1: *Python variables*

We learned how to install Python, its different modules, and now we can start with the actual programs and different basic concepts of Python which can be useful as we go further. Following are the commands you can use to get familiar with programming in Python:

```
python --version
```

```
Python
```

```
[Pradumnas-MacBook-Pro:Desktop pradumnap$ python --version
Python 2.7.14 :: Anaconda, Inc.
[Pradumnas-MacBook-Pro:Desktop pradumnap$ python
Python 2.7.14 |Anaconda, Inc.| (default, Dec  7 2017, 11:07:58)
[GCC 4.2.1 Compatible Clang 4.0.1 (tags/RELEASE_401/final)] on darwin
Type "help", "copyright", "credits" or "license" for more information.
>>>
```

Figure 1.6: *Python console/interactive mode*

Simply, python will redirect you to the Python console/interactive mode, which allows interactive testing and debugging:

1. **Interactive mode programming:**

```
>>>
>>> print ("*********Hello All, We are starting with Python Programming.*********")
*********Hello All, We are starting with Python Programming.*********
>>>
```

Figure 1.7: *Console/ Interactive Mode*

2. **Script mode programming:**

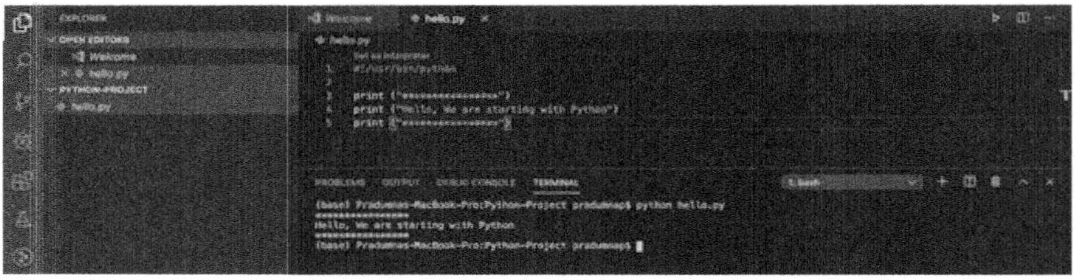

Figure 1.8: *VS IDE for Python programming*

We have mentioned the interpreter in the code so we can run the program as follows:

```
chmod +x hello.py
```

```
./hello.py
```

1.9.2 Python identifier

A Python identifier is a name used to identify a variable, function, class, module, or other object. An identifier should start with an upper or lowercase alphabet, an underscore (_) followed by zero or more letters, underscores, and digits (0 to 9).

Python doesn't support some special characters such as **@, $, %** within identifiers. Python is a case sensitive language so there is a difference in 'Language' and 'language' in Python.

There are many reserved words in Python. The following table lists some of these different reserved keywords:

pass	finally
class	try

def	return
del	with
else	yield
except	global

Table 1.2: *Python reserved words*

1.9.3 Indentation

In Python, spaces and tabs are very important, as incorrect usage can give indentation errors while compiling. The spaces/tabs should be at the same number in the code everywhere. In the following example we can see a for loop print statement which we have given after a tab in the 2nd line, and in first line we have given no spaces or tab. So it will create errors:

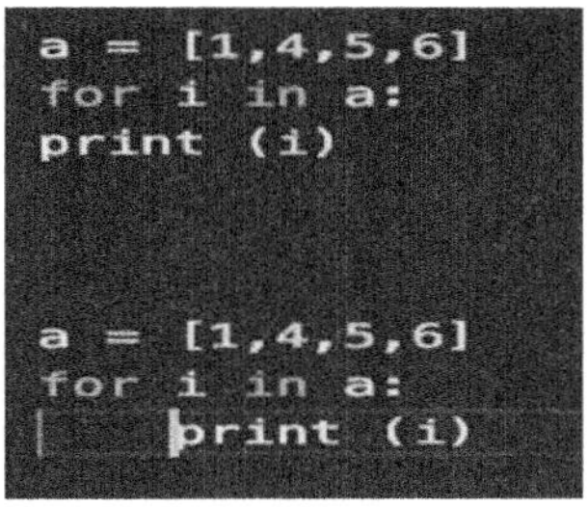

Figure 1.9: *Indentation part*

Comments in Python

We can pass comments in Python as follows:

```
#!/usr/bin/python
```

```
# Comment
print ("Hello,Welcome to Python!")
```

Triple quotes can be used for commenting multiple lines:

```
```
Lines
Xxxxxxx
```
```

1.9.4 Data types in Python

Data type is the format in which the data is stored in the memory. In programming we use data types to instruct and store the data in a particular way such as integers, strings, and more. Following are the standard data types in Python:

- **Integer**: Integers are numeric values. It does operations in the following way:

    var = 1

```
[>>> var=1
[>>> var1=2
[>>> print (var1)
2
[>>> del var1
[>>> print (var1)
Traceback (most recent call last):
  File "<stdin>", line 1, in <module>
NameError: name 'var1' is not defined
>>>
```

Figure 1.10: Integer declaration

In the above example you can see that we have created the variables **var** and **var1**, which we have printed and deleted right after. Python supports different numeric types as well like **int**, **float**, **long**, and **complex**:

int	long	float	Complex
1	-4T42332	1.6	5.65j
49	0L65	89.3	15.6j
111	0x423	-54e	x+yj

Table 1.3: Python numeric Types

- **String**: String in Python is basically a set of characters which is passed between quotation marks. Python supports both double and single inverted quotation marks as shown in *figure 1.11*:

```
[>>>
[>>> st = "Double inverted Commas"
[>>> st1 = 'Single inverted commas'
[>>> print (st)
Double inverted Commas
[>>> print (st1)
Single inverted commas
>>>
```

Figure 1.11: Sting operations

- **List**: List is similar to an array in C which combines strings and integers and is passed between square brackets. Only difference between list and array is that items in a list can be of different data types. Items can be accessed from the list using an index. An example of a list is shown in *figure 1.12*:

```
[>>>
[>>> data = [1, 'pp', 'array', '124']
[>>> print (data)
[1, 'pp', 'array', '124']
[>>> print data[1]
pp
[>>> print data[3]
124
>>>
```

Figure 1.12: List operations

- **Tuples**: Basically a tuple is an immutable sequence object. It is the same as a list however; its values cannot be changed once assigned. Tuples are enclosed in parentheses **( )** instead of square brackets **[ ]** like lists:

```
[>>>
[>>> tp = ('book', 32423, 'line', 43432.34)
[>>> print (tp)
('book', 32423, 'line', 43432.34)
[>>> print tp[3]
43432.34
>>>
```

Figure 1.13: Tuple operations

- **Dictionary**: Dictionary is a hash formatting data type. It has a set of keys and each key has a value format. It is used in many data set operations which show the identity of the user's data. It is closed within curly brackets **{}** and its values can be accessed through square brackets **[ ]**.

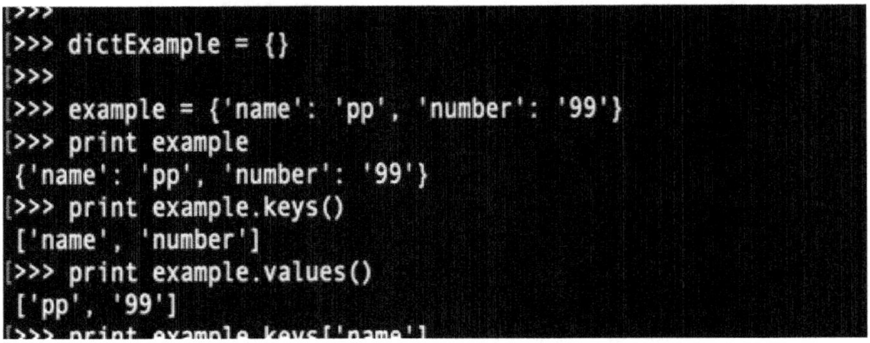

```
>>>
>>> dictExample = {}
>>>
>>> example = {'name': 'pp', 'number': '99'}
>>> print example
{'name': 'pp', 'number': '99'}
>>> print example.keys()
['name', 'number']
>>> print example.values()
['pp', '99']
>>> print example keys['name']
```

Figure 1.14: *Dictionary operations*

1.9.5 Operators in Python

In Python different operators are used to do arithmetic operations like addition, multiplication, etc. Python supports the following operator types:

- Comparison operators

- Logical operators

- Arithmetic operators

There are many more operators in Python. Let's take a look at operators in the following example:

- **Arithmetic operators**: We can use arithmetic operators to do operations on numbers:

  x = 10

  y =6

  x+y =16

  So we can do any operations like addition as well as taking **mod**.

- **Assignment operators**: In this particular example we will assign a value to the variables x, y, and z:

```
[>>>
[>>> x = 10
[>>> y = 3
[>>> z = x + y
[>>> print (z)
13
>>>
```

Figure 1.15: *Assignment operators*

So in the above example we have assigned a value to **z** variable.

- **Comparison operators**: We use comparison operators to compare the values of different data types for different operations. Following is a list of different operators in Python:

    o == Equal to

    o != Not Equal to

    o < Less than

    o Greater than

1.9.6 Loops in Python

We can use loops in Python to perform condition checks and further operations. A loop is used to give control over to a program to do more complex operations depending on the conditions. Python supports the following loop commands:

- **For**: Used for executing multiple times.

- **While**: It tests the condition before executing a loop.

- **Nested**: Contains multiple **for** or **while** loops inside. In complex problem situations, nested loops can be used for validating conditions.

The following diagram represents the structure of a **for** and **while** loop:

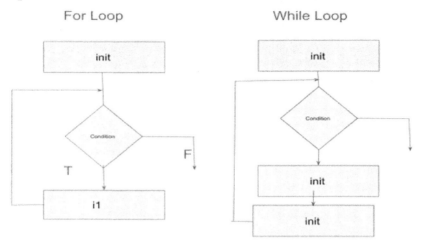

Figure 1.16: *Loops in Python*

The following loop control statements are present:

- **Pass**
- **Break**
- **Continue**

1.9.7 Decision making

In the day to day life we come across many situations where we have to make decisions based on a variety of conditions. To solve such problems in real time programming, conditional statements are used. Following are the conditional statements supported in Python:

- **if** statement
- **if..else** statement
- Nested **if** statements

When we solve conditional statements, we prepare a flow chart to verify the conditions. The following is an example of different conditional statements:

- In *figure 1.17*, we can see that the conditional statement has a single condition with a value assigned to the variable. It means that the conditional statement will first check the value in the compare format and if the condition is met then it will print the value assigned to the variable **con**:

```
>>>
>>> con = 10
>>> if ( con > 5 ):
...     print (con)
...
10
>>>
>>>
>>>
```

Figure 1.17: *if statement*

- In *figure 1.18*, we can see the Boolean condition check where if the values match then the result is either true or false. In this conditional check the value is not of much importance, what's important is the successful condition check:

```
>>>
>>> con = 10
>>> if ( con > 5 ):
...     print True
... else:
...     print Fale
...
True
>>>
```

Figure 1.18: *if…else statement*

1.9.8 Functions/classes/module/ packages in Python

Python supports functions, classes, and modules in a rich manner.

- **Function**: It contains reusable code blocks for better organizing the code. There are many built-in functions in Python like **print()**, **len()**, etc.

  A function start with the **def** keyword. It returns the expression.

  For example,

  ```
  def demo(parameter):
      print ("something")
      #do some operations
      return  expression.
  demo(parameter)
  ```

- **Classes**: Python supports object-oriented programming language and Python is object with its properties and methods so it supports classes.

  For example,

  ```
  class Chapter:
    def __init__(self, name, pages):
      self.name = name
      self.pages = pages
  p1 = Chapter("Nodejs", 70)
  print(p1.name)
  print(p1.pages)
  ```

- **Modules**: It is used for grouping logical code. We can use/ import this code in other files. Hence, it is a collection of functions.

- **Packages**: A collection of modules is called a package.

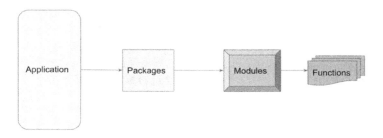

Figure 1.19: *Python code hierarchical design*

Files operations in Python

We can do file operations with the help of Python. There is a built-in function **Open()** to read/write operations in the file. In a file function, you need to pass the following objects:

- File name
- Access mode like **rw, r, a, wa+**, etc.
- Buffering mode

Here, we have seen many aspects of Python programming and there is so much more to learn. We have shared the references for future learning in Python, so you can explore the beauty of Python programming in every field.

1.10 Conclusion

As there are many different use cases of Python programming, we can use Python in many real time applications and projects. Python has a variety of rich modules which can be easily utilized by multiple domains. Python's capacity and power has already been displayed to the industry in all manners of automation. In the next chapter we will cover different use cases of Python and some more syntax.

Points to remember

- Python basic terminologies
- List, dictionary, and tuples
- Python editors
- Python indentation
- The installation process of Python varies across operating systems

Questions and answers

1. **What kind of language is Python?**

   Python is an interpreted language.

2. **When was Python introduced as an official language?**

   1991

3. **What are the main uses of Python?**

   Web development, AI programming, and automation.

4. **What operating systems can Python run on?**

   Linux, Windows, OSx

5. **What is the current version of Python?**

   3.7.x & 3.9.0

Key terms

- **Interpreted language**: It is a programming language which can be directly interpreted without compiling a program into machine instructions.

- **Data type (list, dict, tuple)**: These are the main data types used in Python to play around and do various operations.

- **Indentation error**: It is very important to have indentation errors to look while writing code in Python.

- **All OS support**: It has all main operating system support like Linux and Windows.

CHAPTER 2
Use Cases of Python

2.1 Introduction

Python is a versatile language in terms of automation and many more. In the last chapter we took a look at the history and basics of Python, its syntax, and the capabilities of the Python language.

2.2 Structure

In this chapter we will focus on the following topics from an industrial point of view:

- Features of Python
- Use cases of Python
- Learn more about Python syntax

2.3 Objective

In general, Python is a just language. We can use other languages as well, but Python can be more useful and its beauty of coding is what has caused a gradual adoption from the automation industry and others.

2.4 Features of Python

Python has many features top other programming languages. It doesn't need to provide the type of variable while declaring.

For example:

```
var = 40.
```

Here **var** can be anything, an **int**, **string**, etc.

- **Open source and free**: As Python is open source, anyone can contribute and make it user-friendly. It has a mutual forum where everyone can contribute and provide solutions to a variety of problems. It is ideal for developers as well as for different applications and product development. Python offers an easy and comfortable environment for all kinds of development.

- **High portability**: This feature is especially useful from a developer's point of view as developers may write code on different operating system like Windows, Mac, or Linux. If the code needs to verified or checked on a different operating system, it can be easily done. There is no need to change the code. Hence, Python is one of the most portable languages in the industry.

- **Practical and easy to code**: Python is very easy to code and easy to maintain as compared to other programming languages. It requires less time to learn as compared to other programming languages such as Java, C++, etc.

- **High-level and object-oriented**: As Python is a high-level programming language, we need to bother about the system architecture, its memory configurations. As it supports object-oriented programming, its key feature in the development cycle.

- **Support for GUI**: GUI support is one of the key aspects as the results are more visual. GUI can be imported easily in Python.

- Common key features are as follows:

  o Rich and large standard libraries.

  o Extensible features (can write some Python code in the C or C++ language and also compile that code in C/C++ language)

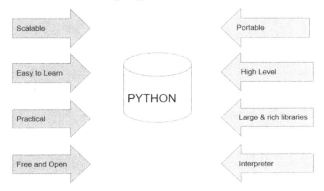

Figure 2.1: Feature lists for Python

2.5 Use cases of Python

Following are the few use cases in a non-real environment from a developer's point of view:

- **Network programming**: Paramiko

- **DevOps and system administrator**: Ansible, OpenStack, Salt

- **Web scraping**: Selenium, Spider

- **Machine learning**: Pandas, IPython, NumPy

  It's scientific and numeric use cases include:

- **Web development**: Django, Bottle, Flask

- **GUI development**: PyGtk, PyQt

- **Testing environment**: Nosetest, Selenium

- **Game development**: PyGame

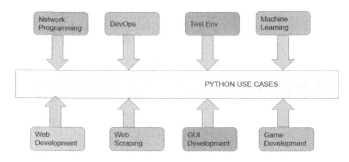

Figure 2.2: Python use cases.

The following four use cases are predominantly practiced in the real world:

- **Web scraping:** It is a data mining or data extraction process in which data from different websites is extracted and stored into a local system or database. Web scraping is also known as crawling or spidering.

  Web scraping can be done with the help of programming and using small pieces of codes/functions which are known as scrapers.

  This use case dominates the industry and is used by many companies like Google to gather information available in the open-source market.

- **Web development:** Python is used for developing web-based real-time server-side applications. In this case we need to use an exact web framework; there are many libraries in Python that we can use to develop web applications. Python is very popular for web development as well.

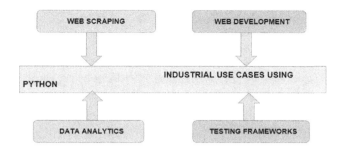

Figure 2.3: *Python industrial use cases*

- **Data analytics:** There are many tools available in Python which can be extensively used for data analysis. It is used for importing excel to any other analysis of data. So nowadays it is easy to analyze data and generate useful charts. Python is best used for analysis work using the R tool. It can be easily used for manipulating the combination of R with Python.

- **Testing framework:** As a developer writes the code, there arises a need for an automated testing framework. Python helps in designing automated test frameworks. Some frameworks are version specific like Robot supports Python 2.7 and above. There are again unit and integrated test cases present; we can write both of these test cases with the help of Python.

Following are the few domains in which Python is used predominantly:

- **Aerospace**: In this industry, it is essential to use travel data to analyze and create meaningful data.

- **Banking**: In banking, data related to banking resources is gathered and processed. Storing this data securely is very crucial.

- **Finance**: In the financial domain, web crawling and data analysis tools are widely used and have already been adapted.

- **Medical**: There is a need for data analysis for different data sets like congresses, patents, researcher publications, etc. in the medical industry.

2.6 Python syntax few more details

Syntax is a structured way of representing logic in programming. Python has its own rules for coding structure and rules. Python was initially designed for limited purposes, however as people realized the advantages of Python and its ease of syntax, its usage began to increase. If the code is clean, then it looks like a complete pseudo code:

```
# Declare and assign value to the variable
i = 10

# Create empty dictionary and list
d = {}
l = []

for j in range(10):
    print (j)
```

Figure 2.4: *Code syntax snippet*

Using *figure 2.4* as an example, we will learn a few details about the syntax. The following points should be kept in mind when you're coding in Python:

- **Indentation for code lines:** In the above example it is clear that there are proper white spaces for print statements.

- **Version-wise difference in Python 2.x and 3.x:** If Python 3.x is used, then the print statement will be a function whereas in Python 2.x it will be a straightforward statement such as: `print j`

- **Commenting statement, statements:** Following are the examples for multiline and single line comments:

```
# This is also commented for single line
```

Figure 2.5: *Multiline commenting*

```
'''
Any thing written inside this will be consider as comment.
'''

'
```

Figure 2.6: Single line comment

- **End of line terminates statement:** If a line is extending and is unable to view properly in the window, then we can use \ for breaking the statement to the next line.

```
# \ is used to break the statement to next line

version = subprocess.Popen(['sh', '/opt/IBM/WebSphere/AppServer/bin/versionInfo.sh'], \
stderr=subprocess.PIPE, stdout=subprocess.PIPE).communicate()[1].decode('UTF-8')
```

Figure 2.7: Line breaker

- **Semicolon is used to terminate statements, but it is completely optional:** Any statement in Python can be terminated by adding a semicolon at the end:

```
Var = 10;

print (j);
```

- **Spaces in a single statement doesn't matter**

```
var=10
var = 10
var =10
# or
a + b =c
a+b =    c
|
```

Figure 2.8: Spaces in the same line

- **Parentheses are for grouping and calling:** Any function is getting called with Parentheses.

2.7 Conclusion

In this chapter we have covered different real-world use cases of Python. We learned that it is very important to have basic knowledge about Python as a programmer and as a technologist. In the next chapter we will cover Python automation, design, and tools as seen in different industries.

Points to remember

- Advanced syntax of Python

- Use cases of Python automation

- Different features of Python

Questions and answers

1. **Is Python an open-source programming Language?**

   Yes, it is.

2. **Are there any arithmetic libraries that are present in Python?**

   Yes.

3. **What are the different use cases of Python?**

   Network programming, GUI/Web development, DevOps tools

Key terms

- **Use cases**: Python has different use cases like Network programming, GUI/UI development, machine learning, DevOps tools, etc.

- **Features**: It has a variety of features such as object-orientation, high-programming language, and support for GUI.

- **Commenting syntax**: It supports single line and multiple line comments in its syntax.

- **Indentation**: This is very important while coding in Python.

CHAPTER 3

Automation Using Python

3.1 Introduction

So far, we have learned the basics of Python with use cases and basic syntax. So we have some hands-on on experience with Python. Now we will go more towards the uses of Python in automation and its different aspects. We will also learn about the Selenium architecture.

3.2 Structure

In this chapter we will focus on automation use cases and design patterns. We will learn about the uses of Selenium in Python automation. Now we will see how Python is useful for automation in various fields:

- Automation use cases

- Design aspects of Python automation

- Use of Selenium in automation

3.3 Objective

Python automation can help improve efficiency and the overall performance of a business. Gradually we will cover the various design aspects and structural aspects of Python and its use cases in the automation industry.

3.4 Automation use cases

- Hardware automation

- Consulting services through web development automation

- Healthcare automation

- Aerospace automation

There are a wide range of use cases for automation. Python is very useful for automation as it gives tests easily and quickly. While writing code in Python, we should follow some standards. Python supports **PEP (Python Enhancement Proposal)** rules.

What PEP does is that it sets the rules for the coder; this helps the code become more readable, more uniform, and predictable as well.

Advantages of automaton

- Accuracy

- Time saving

- Consistency

- Low technical barrier

- Reliability

- Productivity

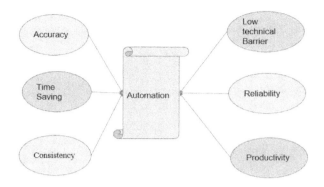

Figure 3.1: Automation benefits

3.5 Design aspects of Python automation

Basically working on automation is fun. Due to this the automation process attracts new users with its ability to save time. Python automation helps the industry/development for testing which enhances the speed of testing. This helps improve the overall output.

The software is designed in unique patterns so whenever we code, we need to follow a specific design pattern. Many people love to code in Python because of its clear syntax, well-structured modules, and packages; this offers enormous flexibility as well as a range of modern features.

It is not compulsory in Python to write complex code such as classes. To reduce complexity, one can simply code with functions only. Rather more simple way like script as well.

We can simply open a terminal, write a simple script, make it executable, and run. In this way you don't even need an IDE or a framework.

Similarly as Python supports object-orientation, functions write as objects completely. Due to Python's flexibility, there are various rules and regulations for structuring the code. Design patterns are basically used to solve well-known issues in real time using proper programming standards.

For example, if anything looks like a **cat** and it does **mauw** then it's a **cat**.

According to this example we specifically try to give an object some features and assign an attribute to that object. On the basis of its attributes we can finalize its type:

```
try:
    animal.mauw()
Except AttributeError:
    self.lol()
```

In the above code you can see that the **animal** attributes are assigned accordingly, and we can conclude the **animal** type. In this code we haven't used an interface like Java and other programming language.

Following are the few patterns in Python:

- Behavioral pattern
- Creational pattern
- Structural pattern

3.5.1 Behavioral pattern

It is one of the first patterns to design and solve complex problems. Behavioral patterns offer repeatable solutions to commonly occurring problems. It involves the following methods:

- Iterators
- Observers
- Templates
- Visitors
- Commands

So it will point to common communication patterns in objects.

3.5.2 Creational pattern

For this type of pattern class and objects, creational pattern is a major criterion. Class Creational patterns use inheritance and object creational pattern users' delegation. It builds different patterns using the following features:

- Builder method

- Abstraction method

- Prototype method

3.5.3 Structural designing pattern

In this a large number of classes and objects are organized in a specific structure. This structure is efficient as well as flexible. It has the following features:

- Decorators

- Composites

- Proxy

- Bridge

In this all design patterns are combined the all Python use case in practical scenarios. So they have their specific manner requirements, and this is fulfilled with the help of their functionality. The advantages of using this design pattern are:

- Efficient development

- Reusability so development is fast

- Transparency

Selenium is used for web application testing and is very useful for browsing data collections. Its major advantage is that it's free and requires no additional licenses. It is supported on all web browsers and only needs a web driver. (Google Chrome, Safari, Firefox, IE, etc.)

3.5.4 Selenium webdriver architecture

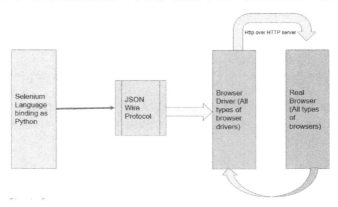

Figure 3.2: Selenium webdriver architecture

The Selenium browser has the following four components:

- **Client library**: Selenium supports multiple libraries like Python, Java, C++, etc.

- **JSON wire protocol**: It is used to transfer data between the server and the client on web. It is a REST API which transfers over an HTTP protocol.

- **Browser driver**: Each browser contains a separate browser driver, and it communicates with the respective drivers.

- **Browser**: It supports multiple browsers as mentioned earlier.

```
WebDriver driver = new FirefoxDriver();
driver.get(https://www.google.com)
```

Figure 3.3: Selenium example code

Here the Firefox web driver and its example have been shown.

3.6 Conclusion

In this chapter we have mainly focused on automation use cases in different industries. We covered basic ideas about design patterns in Python, which are mostly used for automation. We also learned about the Selenium tool and its uses in the industry.

In the next chapter we will learn about industrial automation use cases using Python. We will also explain different scenarios using Raspberry Pi. In the next chapter we will learn in detail about the Raspberry Pi structure and some of its internals as well.

Points to remember

- Automation aspect in the industry
- Automation use cases
- Automation tools
- Web crawling automation tool
- Design patterns in Python

Questions and answers

1. **Which tool is used for automation in Python?**

   Selenium

2. **Is Python used for automation?**

   Yes

3. **What is Selenium?**

   It is a portable framework for testing automation.

Key terms

- **Automation**: It is a process to get tasks done with minimal human input.
- **Types of automation**: Types of automation involve the hardware, different instrumental, software, etc.
- **Python automation**: It involves automation of different software systems and different parts like crawling.
- **Selenium**: It is an automation tool in Python.

CHAPTER 4
Industrial Automation Python

4.1 Introduction

Python is used in a variety of ways in the automation industry. It has various use cases that helps the industry become fast, efficient, and effective. Python can be used to code for system level programming as well. It is used for board level programming as well and makes the application automation for the industry. In this automation, Raspberry Pi is also getting used to make automatic systems.

In this chapter, we will take a look at few examples such as traffic signal monitoring and water level indicators. We will cover the above two examples in detail which are used for industry.

4.2 Structure

This chapter will focus on the following topics which will have more about the example for automation use cases:

- Traffic signal monitoring
- Water level indicator
- Raspberry-Pi board details

4.3 Objective

Industrial automation requires a combination of hardware and software using Python. We will gradually learn the process with the help of the following examples.

4.4 Traffic signal monitoring

In big cities, traffic varies according to the daytime. In monitoring one sided traffic will towards the office location and evening it will be towards the home location.

So the traffic signal should also change accordingly, its time slap changes according to the daytime. We can recreate the above use case with the help of a Raspberry-Pi board. Programming will be in the form of Python.

Architecture

In this example, the heart will be the Raspberry Pi piped to GPIO pins for operating the board. It sends single to the respective LEDs. In the following diagram we can see how the Raspberry Pi operates 4 signals from the chowk according to the day time and how it switches accordingly to the time slot for the signal:

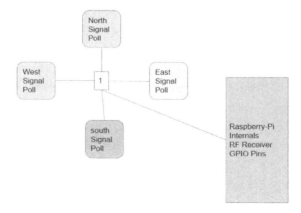

Figure 4.1: Traffic signal architecture

In this particularly, it will be on the signal in a particular direction where the traffic is heavy, the signal green will turn for a longer time and less traffic where the red signal will be turned on for a longer time in the morning. Similarly, in the evening, the reverse will happen. So this system can be used for efficient traffic management in most of real time scenarios. Hence, this time-based traffic management system is dependent on the density of traffic in the city area.

This project is based on a combination of hardware and software (Python programming):

- **Hardware:**
  - o Raspberry Pi board
  - o LEDs
  - o RF transmitter and receiver
- **Software**
  - o Python programming

4.5 Water level controller

In this water level controller, it will provide the information about different water levels indicating their different indications.

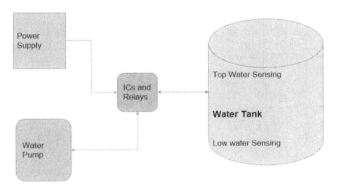

Figure 4.2: High water sensing - Low water sensing

Hardware part

In this specifically, two sensors are present—one is being used to measure the surrounding pressure and the other for measuring the actual water container pressure, the end goes into the under water. The pressure level indicates the depth of water. There are two different pressure levels—one indicates the actual water pressure and the other one indicates the pressure gain from the resistance for the same.

Here the resistance can be caused due to different reasons. In this case resistance is assumed to be constant, because it is getting subtracted. It mostly depends on humidity which remains constant for a certain period of time. There must be a pressure difference in the water pump.

In the following section, I will give a basic Raspberry Pi example for a water level controller. As Raspberry Pi is a small digital computer, it only processes digital signals. So whenever we need to process through it, we will need an analog to digital convertor (ADC).

There are many types of ADC available in the market. In this example we have used MCP3008 as an ADC chip. This chip is common and highly-recommended because it is cheap and requires no additional components.

We will be more precise about voltage levels during all of these activities, as it may cause issues with the Raspberry Pi board. We have to connect the GND of the sensor to 0V and VCC to 3.3V, these are the standards.

Overall connection diagram and circuit diagram is shown in *figure 4.3*:

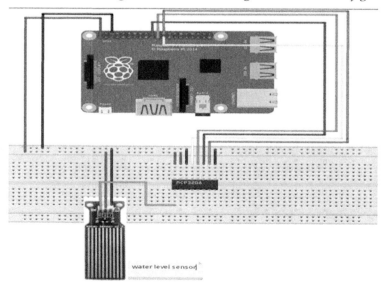

Figure 4.3: *Connection diagram from water level controller*

In the following section, we will learn more about Raspberry Pi.

Raspberry Pi i/p pins are located in the upper left corner of the board as seen in *figure 4.4*. These pins are a combination of voltage supplies, ground, and GPIO (general purpose input/output) pins. You can distinguish them from the following graph:

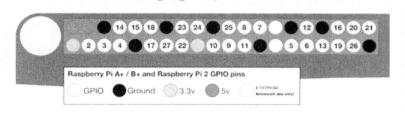

Figure 4.4: *GPIO pin details*

- GPIO pins are your standard pins that are simply used to turn devices on and off. For example, an LED.

- I²C (Inter-Integrated Circuit) pins allow you to connect and talk to hardware modules that support the I2C protocol. This typically requires 2 pins.

- SPI (Serial Peripheral Interface Bus) pins can be used to connect and talk to SPI devices. Pretty much the same as I2C but SPI makes use of a different protocol.

- UART (Universal asynchronous receiver/transmitter) are the serial pins used to communicate with other devices.

- DNC stands for do not connect, this is pretty self-explanatory.

The power pins pull power directly from the Raspberry Pi. GND pins are used to ground your devices. It doesn't matter which pin you use as they are all connected to the same line.

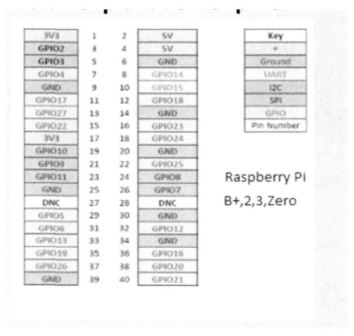

Figure 4.5: *Raspberry Pi pin details.*

Software

You can choose to connect your Raspberry Pi to a monitor, or login in to Raspberry Pi via SSH. This section is divided in the following three parts:

Write the code

Add a new file named **testLevel.py** under the **/home/pi** file path via the Nano editor (the name is arbitrary):

```
sudo nano testlevel.py
```

Write the sample code in a new file, the code can be obtained by executing shell commands:

```
import RPi.GPIO as GPIO

import time
```

```
# change these as desired - they're the pins connected from
the
# SPI port on the ADC to the Cobbler
# photoresistor connected to adc #0
photo_ch = 0
#port init
def init():
        GPIO.setwarnings(False)
        GPIO.cleanup()                  #clean up at the end
of your script
        GPIO.setmode(GPIO.BCM)          #to    specify   which
pin numbering system
        # set up the SPI interface pins
        GPIO.setup(SPIMOSI, GPIO.OUT)
        GPIO.setup(SPIMISO, GPIO.IN)
        GPIO.setup(SPICLK, GPIO.OUT)
        GPIO.setup(SPICS, GPIO.OUT)
         #read SPI data from MCP3008(or MCP3204) chip,8
possible adc's (0 thru 7)
def readadc(adcnum, clockpin, mosipin, misopin, cspin):
#logic for the Analog to digital converter came into picture.
#This is the main function where readadc() function is
getting called.
def main():
        init()
        time.sleep(5)
        while True:
                adc_value=readadc(photo_ch, SPICLK, SPIMOSI,
SPIMISO, SPICS)
                if adc_value == 0:
                        print"no water\n"
                elif adc_value>0 and adc_value<30 :
                        print"it is raindrop\n"
                elif adc_value>=30 and adc_value<200 :
```

```
                    print"it is water flow"
                 print"water level:"+str("%.1f"%(adc_
value/200.*100))+"%\n"
                 #print "adc_value= " +str(adc_value)+"\n"
                 time.sleep(1)
     if __name__ == '__main__':
        try:

            main()


        except KeyboardInterrupt:
            pass
GPIO.cleanup()
```

Execute Python program

```
sudo python ./testLevel.py
```

Test

In the test part, we have to put the sensors into a container by ensuring that the water does not exceed the max height. So as water indicates it depends on the water level inside the container. If there is no water it will show no water and as water increases it will start showing the water level.

4.6 Conclusion

In this chapter we have mainly focused on different real-life use cases of automation in Python. In the next chapter we will learn about web scraping, how it works, and its benefits.

Points to remember

- Industrial use cases of Python

- Main role of Python in automation

- Different examples of Python automation like traffic signal automation and water level indicator

- Raspberry Pi board details

Question and answers

1. **What are the examples of Python automation?**

    Traffic signal automation and water level indicator.

2. **Are there any arithmetic libraries that are present in Python?**

    Yes.

Key terms

- Industrial example: Water level indicator and traffic signal.

- Raspberry Pi board: With the help of a Raspberry Pi board and Python we can demonstrate the various use cases of automation.

- Sample code for water level indicator with detailed hardware and software.

CHAPTER 5
Web Scraping

Introduction

In the last chapter we learnt about Python, its industrial use cases, and its importance in various fields. We explained the software and hardware roles with real-life examples. In this chapter we will mainly focus on web scraping. We will learn how web scraping is important and its various features.

Python is one of the most powerful tools for web scraping. We will cover how Python is used to extract data. We will also see the difference between a scraper and a crawler.

Structure

We will cover the following topics in this chapter:

- Web scraping

- Importance and use cases of web scraping

- Different aspects of web scraping

- Difference between scraper and crawler

- How web scraping works?

- Different types of web scrapers

Objective

Web scraping is used to improve industrial efficiency by extracting more details using a scraper. This data can be transformed from a website into a structured format which is very much useful for further operation and storage point of view.

5.1 Web scraping

Initially people used to crawl (collect information) manually, which was a very slow and time consuming process. People get engaged in the same tasks for many days. So after this efficiency for data collection is increased. In some cases it is easy to get structured data from websites, but if the data format/type is different then it's not as straight forward a process to extract data.

Web scraping is commonly used to extract information from different websites. It extracts data which has not been formatted, very poorly structured from the websites. Before web scraping was not able to directly put data into an Excel which could lead to manual errors.

These manual errors have now been minimized or rather eliminated since web scraping has become more functional and accurate at storing data in different structures and formats; this allows further operations based on the provided structured data.

In this process many Python libraries are also involved directly so that data can be structured using simplified code. To write software for data extraction or crawling, some basic knowledge of HTML, DOM, and other programming languages is a must.

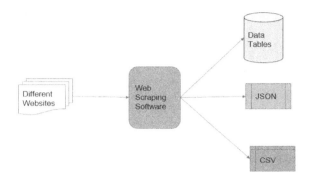

Figure 5.1: *Web scraping*

Following facts should be taken into consideration for web scraping:

- Read through the target website's terms and conditions to understand how you can legally use the data. Most websites prohibit you from using their data for commercial purposes.

- Make sure you are not downloading data at too rapid a rate because this may break the website. You could potentially get blocked from the website as well.

5.2 Importance and use cases of web scraping

Web scraping is rapidly growing in all industries such as medical, marketing, tourism, and many more. So this extracted, crawled data analysis importance also is grown up very fastly. So those are all data used for data science, data journalism as well.

As we can see in *figure 5.2*, information is not limited to a single field. In all fields, information spreads out. With the help of web crawling, we can extract, manage, and analyze this data and present it in a manner that is useful to the common user.

Web scraping is useful for both professional and personal use. Following are the popular use cases of web scraping:

- **Machine learning:** It is part of artificial intelligence where the huge data and data sets need to be fed initially to work proper AI. Proper data needs to be collected and arranged in an appropriate manner before feeding it to the system.

On that data it would create an efficient, workable, and appropriate system.

- **Financial data:** It is very important to get financial market analysis as to grow the world. Web scraping is used to collect proper stock market data for proper analysis.

- **Social media data:** This trend has also increased nowadays to get more useful data from social media to ensure accurate targeted advertising. This is how people get proper recommendations as per their needs on social media.

There are many more use cases that we will cover in the coming topics and chapters while explaining more details about web scraping.

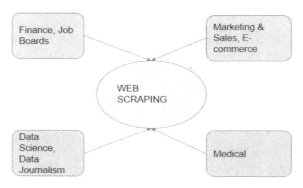

Figure 5.2: Web scraping

Following are two of the most commonly used web scraping techniques:

- **Manual extraction:** This involves manual extraction and arrangement of data from websites. This process is time consuming and inefficient. As this is a manual process, the data can be unreliable as human errors may get introduced.

- **Automated extraction:** Automatic extraction can be possible through the following software methodology:

  o **DOM (Document Object Model) parsing:** It is an interface that is used for modifying and updating the structure and content of XML documents.

  o **HTML parsing:** In this particularly, take the code and extract relevant information as per the point of view of users.

○ **Web scraping software**: Nowadays there are many web scraping software available so directly need to provide the headers as input parameters and automatically relevant data get available in the comfortable format in CSV, JSON. However in some cases it is not possible to provide all the keys, so you need to modify the code for the tool if the tool is open source.

These tools are specifically designed to extract data from the internet. Following are few useful tools for web scraping

- Scrapinghub

- Parsehub

- Import.io

○ **XPath**: Xpath is a query language that works with XML documents. XML has a tree like structure so XPath is getting travel through that tree to get appropriate data. So the various key parameters can be selected while traveling through tree.

○ **Text pattern matching**: This is regular expression pattern matching using the help of **grep** command in the UNIX system.

5.3 Different aspects of web scraping

Before we start with actual web scraping, let's take a look at its two most important parameters:

- Crawler

- Scraper

In the following diagram you can learn about the various differences between web scraping and web crawling:

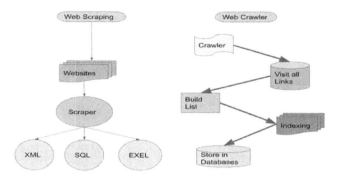

Figure 5.3: Difference in web scraping vs. crawler

5.3.1 Crawler

A crawler browses the internet to index and search relevant content. It gets links in a logical manner. It follows the extra steps for data collection. The extra steps involved are as follows:

- Indexing

- Storing in databases

Stored information in the database can be processed further to showcase on the UI. With the help of that information, application development and product development as well as maintenance get easier.

5.3.2 Scraper

It is a specialized tool used for accurate crawling and extracting data. It gets these values from HTML. It can be used to store data in a particular file format such as JSON, XML, CSV, etc. With the help of a scraper, storing data in a spreadsheet becomes quick and easy. In *figure 5.4*, you can see that the scraper crawls the website and stores the data into a structured file format for easy readability. Scraping is also known as human mining as it generates data which is easy to read.

Figure 5.4*: Aspect of Web scraping*

5.4 How web scraping works?

Over the years websites have gotten more and more complicated, similarly tools used for crawling have become complicated as well. In web scraping the use cases are truly infinite.

As we have discussed, web scraping is the process of extracting data from different websites through an automated software programming script. Hence, this process mainly contains the following three steps:

- **Requesting the content:** In its first step, any web crawling program will request the webpage for their permission to crawl.

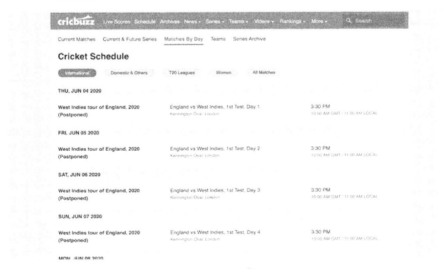

Figure 5.5*: Site*

In this example, the scraper sends a **GET** request to the webpage cricbuzz and gets the schedule for international matches.

- **Extract the data:** In this example, when we try to extract any data, we will inspect the particular element references elements. In this case we crawl the data related to the match type, date, and with whom vs. whom. So to get/extract data we need a parser. Python is useful for writing scripts for parsing.

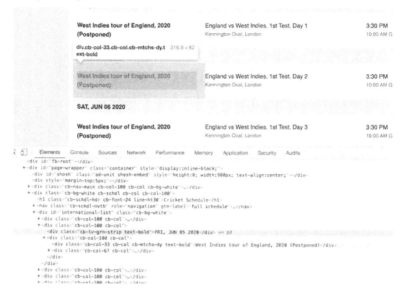

Figure 5.6: Parsing data

- **Store the data:** In the final step, we get the data in a CSV and JSON file as per the convenient format.

This stores the respective information into a CSV or JSON file. The information collected will be useful for further operations. Sometimes this information gets used for UI operations to show. Mostly in the backend developer create the format information in the JSON, so it is easy to operate during showing on UI.

Figure 5.7: CSV format data

In this process many exceptions for the code as well in the web parser may occur, they need to be resolved in an appropriate manner to make the crawler generalized.

5.5 Different types of web scrapers

1. **Scraper API:**

   Scraper API handles proxies, browsers, and CAPTCHAs, so you can crawl the HTML of any web page with a simple API call. Initially 1000 API calls are free, after that charges may be applicable according to your plan.

   Advantages:

   - It can be easily integrated.

   - It can also automate CAPTCHA.

   - JavaScript rendered pages can also be scraped.

   - It will never block by IP or captcha.

   - It is completely customizable.

   - It is fast and reliable.

2. **Web Scraper:**

   This is browser-based and free. It is capable of extracting data from both modern and dynamic websites.

   Advantages:

- Coding is not required
- Cloud Web Scraper
- Scraped data accessible through API

3. **Grasper:**

   Grasper is a SaaS-based web scraping service. It is not free and offers various plans. It is a complete solution for marketers and investors.

   Features:

   - Mostly preferred by investors, pricing seems like crucial information
   - Useful for cleaning marketing data
   - Supports multiple output formats
   - Email delivery

There are many more crawlers available like Scraper and Nutch. Nutch is completely written in Java. It should be noted that search engines are developed using these scrapers.

5.6 Conclusion

In this chapter we covered web scraping and its different types. We also covered different aspects of web scraping. Then we took a look at the difference between a scraper and a crawler, and their various use cases.

Points to remember

- Web scraping
- Use of web scraping
- Aspects of web scraping
- Types of web scraping

Questions

1. Why is web scraping used?

2. What are the differences between web scraping and crawling?

3. What are the areas in which web scraping is used?

Answers

1. Web scraping is used for collecting data.

2. After crawling, data gets stored into a database, whereas in web scraping data is stored in a specific file format such as JSON.

3. Finance, machine learning, and social media

Key terms

-   **Web scraping**: It is used to extract data from websites.

-   **Web crawling**. It is a program or script which systematically browses the web and stores this data into a database.

-   **Uses of web crawling in different domains**: Machine learning, finance, and social media.

Chapter 6
Web Scraping and Its Necessity

6.1 Introduction

In the last chapter we saw the basics of web scraping and web crawling. We also covered the differences between the two and learned when to use web scraping and when to use web crawling. We also learnt how exactly web scraping works using examples.

In this chapter we will take a deep dive into web scraping and learn how we can leverage the same. We will also see why web scraping is essential for modern businesses.

6.2 Structure

We will study the following topics in this chapter:

- Deep dive inside the web scraping
- Necessity of web scraping
- How is web scraping useful for startups?

6.3 Objective

We will learn about search engines and their importance in the industry. Crawled data sets useful for monitoring, comparison, listing, and further operations in different industries.

6.4 Details of web scraping

As we have learned, web scraping means to collect data from websites and store it in a structured and organized manner. In the following example we will go in more detail about web scraping using a Python library. For the following example we will make use of the **BeautifulSoup** library.

You can download this library from the following website, containing names of persons and other details: **https://new.mta.info/ transparency/leadership/past-board-chairs**

From the above link, we will scrape data pertaining to the past MTA board chairs. If you were to do it manually then you'd have to copy everyone's data and store it. Thanks to web scrapers, you can do it in an efficient way. So in the future if you need to perform a similar task, it will be easier and time efficient compared to manual work.

Joseph J. Lhota
Terms: 01/09/2012 to 12/31/2012, and 06/21/2017 to 11/08/2018

Thomas F. Prendergast
Term: 06/20/2013 to 01/31/2017

Jay H. Walder
Term: 10/05/2009 to 10/21/2011

H. Dale Hemmerdinger
Term: 10/22/2007 to 09/10/2009

Peter S. Kalikow
Term: 03/13/2001 to 10/22/2007

E. Virgil Conway
Term: 05/18/1995 to 03/09/2001

Figure 6.1: *Web page to be scraped*

Following facts should be taken into consideration during web scraping:

- Anyone crawling or scraping a website should understand the terms and conditions of the site to avoid legal issues. Sometimes data is completely IP (intellectual property) of the site owner.

- While downloading data from different websites, we should keep the crawling data speed in check as it can break the website content. This can lead the owner of the site to block you if any suspicious activity is detected.

So following are the steps from which web scraping has gone through at every step:

1. **Inspect the website**: When we start crawling a website, the first thing we need is the HTML structure of that website. This includes tags, XPath, etc. So we should use the DOM structure of the site. A basic knowledge of HTML is necessary for getting proper and appropriate data. While crawling a website, right click on the page and click on **Inspect**. This will take us to the raw code structure behind the site:

Figure 6.2: *Inspect the website*

After clicking **Inspect**, we can see the different parameters such as **Elements**, **Network**, and **Console**. This data can be seen in the network as well with API calls. Decide the data that you want to crawl and click on it. Immediately, we will see the HTML tags and its details. So we will get those tags details by crawling:

Figure 6.3: *Array symbol in inspect*

```
<span class="mta-card-title mta-font-bold">Peter S.
Kalikow</span>
```

You will find that **<span>** is used for hyperlinks. Now that we have identified the location from the link, we will begin coding.

2. **Python code**: We will start by importing the following libraries:

```
import requests

import urllib.request

import time

from bs4 import BeautifulSoup
```

Now, we will add the **url** to the website and access the site with our requests library, and see the response:

```
url = 'https://new.mta.info/transparency/leadership/
past-board-chairs'

response = requests.get(url)
```

If the access was successful, you should see the following output:

```
>>> from bs4 import BeautifulSoup

>>> url = 'https://new.mta.info/transparency/
leadership/past-board-chairs'

>>>

>>> response = requests.get(url)

>>>

>>> response

<Response [200]>
```

We will use the method **.findAll** to locate all of the **<a>** tags:

soup.findAll('a')

This code gives us every line of code that contains an `<a>` tag:

```
▼ <a href="/transparency/leadership/past-board-chairs" class="mta-card mta-flex mta-flex-grow mta-flex-col">
    <span style="background-image: url('/sites/default/files/2018-05/lhota.png')" class="mta-flex mta-h-1800 mta-bg-
    card mta-bg-cover bg-no-repeat"></span>
  ▼ <span class="mta-flex mta-flex-grow mta-p-150 mta-pb-250 mta-text-3xl mta-min-h-1200">
    ▼ <span class="mta-card-content mta-relative mta-block mta-w-full">
        <span class="mta-card-title mta-font-bold">Joseph J. Lhota</span>
        <span class="mta-card-subtitle mta-block mta-text-2xl mta-leading-400 mta-font-bold">Terms: 01/09/2012 to
        12/31/2012, and 06/21/2017 to 11/08/2018</span>
      </span>
    </span>
  </a>
```

Figure 6.4

Sample code for downloading images and names:

```python
# Import libraries
import requests
import urllib.request
import time
from bs4 import BeautifulSoup
# Set the URL you want to webscrape from
url = 'https://new.mta.info/transparency/leadership/
past-board-chairs'
# Connect to the URL
response = requests.get(url)
# Parse HTML and save to BeautifulSoup object¶
soup = BeautifulSoup(response.text, "html.parser")
# To download the whole data set, let's do a for loop
through all a tags
line_count = 1 #variable to track what line you are on
for one_a_tag in soup.findAll('a'):  #'a' tags are for
links
    if line_count >= 36: #code for text files starts
at line 36
        link = one_a_tag['href']
            download_url = 'http://web.mta.info/
developers/'+ link
```

```
                      urllib.request.urlretrieve(download_
url,'./'+link[link.find('/turnstile_')+1:])

        time.sleep(1) #pause the code for a sec

   #add 1 for next line

   line_count +=1
```

6.5 Necessity of web scraping

In industry, any problem statement goes through the process of data collection or data processing. In this process, the web scraper plays a very vital role in data analysis. In *figure 6.4*, we can see that initially understanding the concept is very important, after that data information we have to gather. Then a web scraper comes in picture. So everywhere you can see nowadays machines are doing work for humans. A lot of things are getting automated with the help of data:

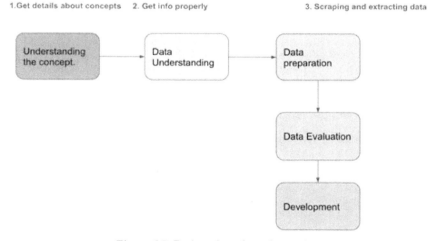

Figure 6.5: Project phase for web scraping

Once you get the desired data, you can analyze the same as per your requirements. So the day to day life importance of web scraping gets increased. In business it has a very large scale use case along with the major importance. So the desired data gets collected and analysis can be done over the period.

Following are the reasons why web scraping is useful for businesses:

* It help with gaining visibility on social media
* Controlling the brand over the internet

- Building an online reputation

- Building a powerful search engine

- Allowing you to make customized data according to your needs

- Allows you to gather all the data in a central location

Following are the reasons due to which web scraping is getting more popular:

- **Speed**: The speed at which we collect data through web scraping is very fast due to automation. In fact as data increases across websites, it becomes more important for scraping tools to become faster. There is no need to keep monitoring, the scraper server gets data in the background at a faster speed.

- **Accuracy**: The data which we collect is more accurate and precise according to the keys/values which we have collected using the scraper.

- **Business information**: As a business grows, the information also grows at a fast speed. The data in the field of sales and marketing has a lot of importance. Web scraping helps get this data and makes analyzing this data easy and efficient.

- **Need data for machine learning modules**: The data is needed for all fields; similarly it has its importance in AI (artificial intelligence). On the basis of huge gathered data, the machines get trained. So to work the machine properly the data should be accurate and speedy. So manual efforts are not useful in this case.

6.6 Deep dive inside the web scraping

While writing a scraper program, the rules are the same. General steps for a scraper program are as follows:

- Write the rules for scraping/extracting specific data

- Pull all the data that you want.

- Copy all data into a single spreadsheet.

Similarly, we can do this with a crawler:

- Write the crawler script

- Pull necessary data from websites

- Dump all necessary data into a database

Following are some common hurdles that you may face while web scraping:

- Most of the websites are simple to crawl

- Sometimes web developers do not follow proper style guides; their code may contain various mistakes.

- Many websites build in HTML 5, so every element is unique.

- Websites have their own encoding sometimes which makes it impossible to send back with request.

As we write our customized scraper program, it is helpful to get closer to 95% accuracy towards the site crawler. The following structure should be followed for customized websites:

- First look at HTML code.

- Next look into the DOM Structure, so target data gets analyzed properly.

In the next step the design of system is done that, there are 3 types of part. One is the default reader, reader, and complex reader. So it depends on the sites which crawler is getting called:

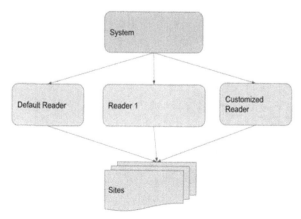

Figure 6.6*: Customized crawler*

6.7 Conclusion

In this chapter we have learnt about the insides and importance of web scraping. In the next chapter we will learn more about different web scraping tools.

Points to remember

- Detailed web scraping procedure
- Necessity of web scraping
- Web scraping is useful for startups

Questions

1. Is basic knowledge of HTML needed for web scraping?
2. What language is used for web scraping?
3. What are the different uses of web scraping?

Answers

1. Yes, a basic knowledge in HTML is needed for web scraping.
2. Python.
3. Useful for startups, accounting, and the medical sector.

Key terms

- **Necessity of web scraping**: Used in different industries for different reasons.
- **Insides of web scraping**: Detailed information about how a web scraper works.

CHAPTER 7

Python Web Scraping and Different Tools

7.1 Introduction

In the last chapter we covered web scraping and how it works. In this chapter, we will focus on how Python is useful for web scraping and the different tools we can use in the web scraping process. We will systematically capture and organize large amounts of data with the help of web scraping and put it into a database.

7.2 Structure

Different tools for web scraping and their limitations

- How easy Python is for web scraping
- Syntax for Python web scraping
- Sample example for web scraping

7.3 Objective

We will learn more about different tools used for web scraping and their uses. We will also get to know about Python syntax in web scraping with examples:

Web scraping tools

Python syntax for web scraping along with examples

7.4 Different tools for web scraping and their limitations

Web scraping can be done using multiple tools and frameworks in Python. There are a variety of options available depending on the target website and your specific needs. Web scraping can automate data extraction using bots. Web crawlers index the information from a webpage using bots.

Following are some of the most popular scraping tools:

Request

Urllib2

Beautiful Soup

Selenium

MechanicalSoup

urllib2 is preinstalled with Python whereas you'll need to install the other tools manually.

Request: It is not pre-installed with Python; we can install Request with the help of **pip**:

pip install requests

```
>>>
>>> import requests
>>> req = requests.get('https://www.berlios.de/linux-fuer-alte-rechner/')
>>> print(req.headers['Content-Type'])
text/html; charset=UTF-8
>>> print(req.history)
[]
```

Figure 7.1: Command for request

urllib2: urllib2 is a Python module used for fetching URLs. Using this different information can be scrapped. It defines the different functions and classes for help. This is used for fetching **urls** with the help of FTP and HTTP. You can see how pages are crawled using Urllib2 in *figure 7.3*.

Figure 7.2: Extraction using Urllib2

Beautiful Soup: It is a parsing library like requests, pcap etc. used to parse different parsers. It creates a parser tree that is used for extracting data from HTML. It automatically converts incoming documents to Unicode and outgoing documents to UTF-8. We can see an example of how this works in *figure 7.4*:

Figure 7.3: Beautiful Soup commands

Lxml: Lxml is a Python library which allows easy handling of XML and HTML files and can also be used for web scraping. It contains many modules such as etree (ElementTree) which is responsible for creating elements and structures using these elements. If your priority is speed, then **lxml** is the perfect choice.

Installation for lxml same as requests module of python as

```
pip install lxml
```

Following is an example of a basic Lxml syntax:

```
>>>
>>> from lxml import etree
>>> root_elem = etree.Element('html')
>>> etree.SubElement(root_elem, 'head')
<Element head at 0x1082fb758>
>>> etree.SubElement(root_elem, 'title')
<Element title at 0x1082fb7e8>
>>> etree.SubElement(root_elem, 'body')
<Element body at 0x1082fb758>
>>> print(etree.tostring(root_elem, pretty_print = True).decode("utf-8"))
<html>
  <head/>
  <title/>
  <body/>
</html>
```

Figure 7.4: *lxml command*

Lxml is basically used for system XML files to crawl and it is helped in different web applications as well to crawl.

Selenium: The Selenium API uses a WebDriver Protocol to control the web browser. The browser can run either locally or remotely. Selenium is really useful when you have to perform different actions on a website such as:

Clicking buttons

Filling forms

Scrolling

Taking a screenshot

You can install Selenium using the following command:

pip install selenium

We can run Selenium in both headful (with content in browser) and headless (without content in browser) mode.

7.5 How easy Python is for web scraping

First, we need to figure out how we can crawl websites from different tags given in the HTML page. To get proper information from crawling, a basic knowledge of HTML tags is a must.

We can provide details to the crawler in the following way:

Right click on the site and click on **Inspect**:

Figure 7.5: *Inspect the elements*

Once you've clicked on **Inspect**, you should see this console pop up:

Figure 7.6: *Inspect console*

If access is successful then you'll see the following output:

```
>>>
>>> r = requests.get('https://www.berlios.de/linux-fuer-alte-rechner/')
>>> print r
<Response [200]>
>>>
```

Figure 7.7: *Response output*

Next, we will parse the HTML page with Beautiful Soup and Selenium.

Locating data on a website is one of the main use cases for Selenium, either for a test suite (making sure that a specific element is present/absent on the page) or for extracting data and saving it for further analysis (web scraping).

7.6 Syntax for Python web scraping with Selenium

There are many methods available in the Selenium API for selecting elements on a page. You can use:

Tag name

Class name

IDs

XPath

CSS selectors

If you're not familiar with XPath, it is a technology that uses path expressions to select nodes or node sets in an XML document (or in our case an HTML document). Even though XPath is not a programming language in itself, it allows you to write expressions that can be used for directly accessing specific HTML elements without having to go through the entire HTML tree.

I am considering that the knowledge of HTML is already there. So you already know that a web page is a document containing web pages with tags in different elements like titles, paragraphs, list, etc.

The following figure will explain the HTML framework. HTML hierarchy can be viewed as a tree. We can see this hierarchy through indentation in the HTML code. When your web browser parses this code, it creates a tree which is an object representation of the HTML document. This is known as the **Document Object Model (DOM)**.

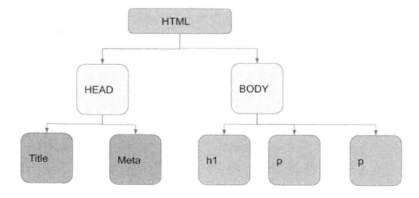

Figure 7.8: *Page description in HTML.*

7.7 Sample example for web scraping

In this section we will see the sample example. In the following example we will see the scraping functionality of site.

From the ESPN website (**http://www.espncricinfo.com/rankings/content/page/211270.html**), we will crawl different types of data such as names, ranks, ratings, country, and more:

```
>>> import requests
>>> from bs4 import BeautifulSoup
>>>
>>> res = requests.get("http://www.espncricinfo.com/rankings/content/page/211270.html")
soup = BeautifulSoup(res.text,"lxml")
## if any different table you expect to have then just change the index number
## and the appropriate name in the selector
item = soup.select("iframe[name='testbat']")[0]['src']
req = requests.get(item)
sauce = BeautifulSoup(req.text,"lxml")
for items in sauce.select("table tr"):
    data = [item.text for item in items.select("th,td")]
    print(data)
>>> soup = BeautifulSoup(res.text,"lxml")
>>>     ## if any different table you expect to have then just change the index number
...     ## and the appropriate name in the selector
...     item = soup.select("iframe[name='testbat']")[0]['src']
>>> req = requests.get(item)
sauce = BeautifulSoup(req.text,"lxml")
for items in sauce.select("table tr"):
    data = [item.text for item in items.select("th,td")]
    print(data)
```

Figure 7.9: *Crawl site and detailed script*

After crawling, we get this data in a table format, as shown in *figure 7.11*:

```
>>>
>>> res = requests.get("http://www.espncricinfo.com/rankings/content/page/211270.html")
soup = BeautifulSoup(res.text,"lxml")
## if any different table you expect to have then just change the index number
## and the appropriate name in the selector
item = soup.select("iframe[name='testbat']")[0]['src']
req = requests.get(item)
sauce = BeautifulSoup(req.text,"lxml")
for items in sauce.select("table tr"):
    data = [item.text for item in items.select("th,td")]
    print(data)
>>> soup = BeautifulSoup(res.text,"lxml")
>>>     ## if any different table you expect to have then just change the index number
...     ## and the appropriate name in the selector
...     item = soup.select("iframe[name='testbat']")[0]['src']
>>> req = requests.get(item)
sauce = BeautifulSoup(req.text,"lxml")
for items in sauce.select("table tr"):
    data = [item.text for item in items.select("th,td")]
    print(data)

>>> sauce = BeautifulSoup(req.text,"lxml")
>>> for items in sauce.select("table tr"):
...     data = [item.text for item in items.select("th,td")]
...     print(data)
...
[u'ICC Player Rankings']
[u'Rank', u'Name', u'Country', u'Rating']
[u'1', u'S.P.D. Smith', u'AUS', u'911']
[u'2', u'V. Kohli', u'IND', u'886']
[u'3', u'M. Labuschagne', u'AUS', u'827']
[u'4', u'K.S. Williamson', u'NZ', u'813']
[u'5', u' Babar Azam', u'PAK', u'800']
[u'6', u'D.A. Warner', u'AUS', u'793']
[u'7', u'C.A. Pujara', u'IND', u'766']
[u'8', u'J.E. Root', u'ENG', u'764']
[u'9', u'A.M. Rahane', u'IND', u'726']
[u'10', u'B.A. Stokes', u'ENG', u'718']
[u'\xa0', u'Top 100']
>>>
```

Figure 7.10: *Crawled data*

7.8 Conclusion

In this chapter, we saw different aspects of web crawling and various tools. We also learnt about web scraping syntax in Python. In the next chapter, we will learn how we can automate scraping and web crawling.

Points to remember

Python web scraping: Scrapes data from different websites and arranges it in a systematic manner.

Syntax of Python for web scraping.

Questions

1. What kind of technical knowledge is needed for web scraping?
2. Which Python version is used for web scraping?
3. Which parsing library is mostly used for web scraping?
4. Is Python useful for web scraping?

Answers

1. Python or any language and basics of HTML.
2. Python version 2.7 onwards.
3. Beautiful Soup
4. Yes, Python is useful for web scraping.

Key terms

- **Different tools for web scraping**: Request, Selenium, etc.
- **Beautiful Soup tool**: One of the useful web data parsing libraries.

CHAPTER 8

Automation in Web Scraping

8.1 Introduction

In the previous chapter, we saw the different tools that we can use for web scraping, how Python is used in web scraping, and an elaborate example for the same. In this chapter, we will learn how we can automate web scraping. We will cover the other importance of web scraping, and its various real-time problem-solving capabilities.

8.2 Structure

- How is web scraping useful for industries?
- How automation works in web scraping
- Examples of web scraping with machine learning

8.3 Objectives

We will learn how automated web scraping is used for solving real world problems and its role in data mining as well other industries.

8.4 Web scraping importance in industry

In the real world whenever we start a business, we need data to build the foundation. In this scenario, web scraping plays a very important role. In any industry, web scraping is getting more and more important.

Following is a list of industries where web scraping is being used. We will cover this in more detail later in the chapter:

E-commerce

Social media

Automobile

Real estate

Startup companies

8.4.1 E-commerce

It is very important to observe your competitors in any industry. In the e-commerce business, on the basis of this data, a company can decide their strategy and gauge the demand for their services or goods in the market. This is why data analysis plays an important role while making strategy decisions. To collect such data for analysis, web scraping plays an important role:

Figure 8.1: *Ecommerce data*

8.4.2 Social media

In social media web scraping plays a key role as data to gather social aspects of media. Most of the social networking websites allow data crawling using **APIs (Application Programming Interface)**. Through web scraping, we can collect details about different users from social media as well as other information as per your requirement.

8.4.3 Automobile

Web scraping is used to collect appropriate information on different vehicles and promotions in the automobile industry. With the help of web scraping, we can predict future trends which allow companies to sustain against their competition.

Automobile companies are looking for following are patterns:

Spare part partners and their information related data to be crawled:

Data on customer habits and preferences

Price comparison between different parts

Automobile Industry

Data from Industrial Input Sites · Data Crawler · Structural Data

Figure 8.2: *Automobile industry*

8.4.4 Real estate

In the real estate business, web scraping is used to collect data such as customer phone numbers, e-mail IDs, and the type of projects or properties people are looking for. As per your requirements, it is important to keep the database ready for all types of data in the real estate domain and send out appropriate add to customers.

8.4.5 Startup companies

Currently many startup companies research and compile data to fix their target audience to build up data and their requirements. As per data collected the startup targets the product development and gives base data as crawled data.

Following diagram shows it in the chart format with all field data:

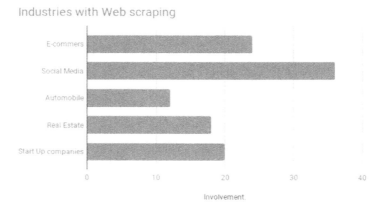

Figure 8.3: Industries involvement in percentage in webs craping

8.5 How automation works in web scraping

Web scraping can solve many real world problems with the help of data collection. It allows us to understand and forecast future demand. In *figure 8.4*, we can see different levels of web scraping and how it has evolved over time. So automatically the effectiveness gets increased and performance also improved in the industries like automobile, real estate etc.

LEVEL OF AUTOMATION

Low			High

Basic WS   Web Crawling   WS with ML   WS with AI

Web Scraping Services

WS: Web Scraping
ML: Machine Learning
AI: Artificial Intelligence

Figure 8.4: *Level of Automation*

It is very important to decide the level of web scraping before you begin a project. Following are the three main levels involved in automated web scraping:

Project decisions determine the websites we need to crawl. This is the primary goal for any core team as the future of all operations is dependent on the data we collect.

Next, we need to parse the collected data from all the web pages. Through automation, we can easily sort this data into different categories such as names, addresses, and more, into a CSV or JSON file.

As per the further operations, data gets processed and stored into databases. All those operations are automated using crawler and its operations are further utilized.

Ultimately, it is possible for any business to automate data collection and parsing to meet their specific goals.

Figure 8.5: *Data crawling*

In *Figure 8.5*, we can see how project decisions turn into data information sources using HTML crawling that is web crawling. We can store this data into a database or CSV file, which is completely structured and useful for future use.

8.6 Web scraping with ML

In the following example, we'll explain the process of web scraping with ML:

Download the page from URL:

```
from urllib.request import urlopen

def download_and_save_page(url, file):
    html_code = urlopen(url).read()#.decode('utf-8')
    f = open(file, 'wb')
    f.write(html_code)
    f.close()
    return html_code
```

Fetch the data from page:

```
links = soup.find_all('a', href=True, class_='car-link')
for link in links:
    print(link['href'])
soup.find('div', class_='car-price').get_text()
df = pd.read_csv('car_data.csv')
```

Car_data.csv file contain Store values scraped for websites.

Finally, we will visualize this data using **ProfileReport** from **pandas-profiling**, a Python module that generates reports from the **pandas DataFrame**. This report gives us a quick visualization of statistics for all the variables in our dataset:

```
from pandas_profiling import ProfileReport

prof = ProfileReport(df)

prof.to_file('output.html')
```

By visualizing this data, we can get a clear comparison between different data sets fetched from the web. Using these data visualizations, ML makes decisions.

8.7 Conclusion

In this chapter we saw some more aspects of web scraping. We have the industry percentages for crawler utilization and their efficiencies.

In the next chapter, we'll take a look at different industrial web scraping examples in more depth.

Points to remember

- Industries details in web scraping.
- Procedure for web scraping.

Questions

1. Which industry is having the highest uses of web scraping?
2. Is web scraping works in ML (machine learning)?

Answers

1. Social media.
2. Yes, web scraping works in ML

Key terms

- **Web scraping used in Industries**: Different percentages in industries.

CHAPTER 9
Use Cases of Web Scraping

9.1 Introduction

In the last chapter we learnt about automation in web scraping. We covered how automation is important regardless of the industry. Now we will see various use cases of web scraping. It is useful for a variety of real-life scenarios and helps enhance both business efficiency and end user support.

9.2 Structure

This chapter will cover various use cases of web scraping. It is not only web scraping but also web content extraction which plays a vital role in the industry.

- Different use cases in web scraping

9.3 Objectives

In this chapter well will get an idea about the various uses of web scraping in the real world. The following topics will be covered in this chapter:

- Technology usage in web scraping

- Speeding up the data information with scrapers

9.4 Different use cases of web scraping

In this section we will be covering the use cases.

9.4.1 Market research

In market research, everything is driven by data. This data should be both accurate and highly informative. It involves different parameters such as:

- Market price

- Research and Development

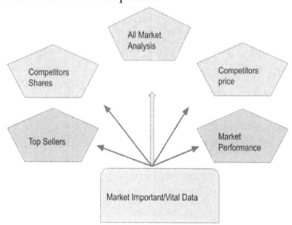

Figure 9.1: *Market analysis*

Market analysis and forecasts are dependent on the quality of data. From *Figure 9.1*, it is clear that market analysis is only as good as the data you collect. To get an accurate reading of the market, data analysis is a very powerful tool.

9.4.2 Medical industry

Nowadays, web scraping is widely used across the medical industry as well. Doctors and patients, both benefit from data collection. Web scraping is being rapidly adopted by the health care industry. In this sector, continuous web scraping and crawling is used by pharmaceutical companies, hospitals, and other health care organizations.

Following steps are generally followed while crawling:

- Selecting the websites from which data is to be crawled.

- Organizing collected data into CSV/JSON files as per your needs.

- Often, custom software is designed to show data for pharmaceutical companies and hospitals. To use that data, first you need to store this data into MongoDB.

In *figure 9.2*, you can see example for data store and representative software:

- Provide websites as an input.
- Crawlers/scrapers will generate JSON/CSV files.
- Databases are used to store this data with maximum usability point of view.
- Write the software.
- Show the data on UI according to the use case of industry.

We can write the ML data sets from that data so that it can be useful for the material point of view in the industry.

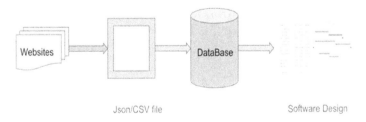

Figure 9.2: *Crawling process*

Some companies design custom software from crawled data and make it available to hospitals as well. For example, Practo is software based on collected data and available for public use to improve end user experience.

When hiring new staff, the following information is useful in the medical industry:

- Name
- Area
- Specialization
- Clinic timings
- Degrees
- Contact information
- Doctor's experience
- Reviews and feedback

1. Different pharmaceutical websites to be crawled.
2. Storing and organizing this data in JSON/CSV format.

***Figure 9.3**: CSV formatted data*

3. Next, these JSON/CSV files are stored into a database so they can be accessed by the software.

4. After successful integration of data into software, companies make the website available for software release.

***Figure 9.4**: Site designed.*

In the above screenshot, we can see the following steps being followed:

1. Data crawled from different websites makes doctors' profiles and information available.

2. It initially collects and saves this data in the CSV/JSON format. (It is part of crawling/scraping)

3. This data is then stored in a database, mostly a NoSQL database where it is easy to format this data.

4. On top of data from the database it is written the well formatted API, so the data can be easily available for the UI representation.

5. In the last phase, we can see this data represented in a UI as shown in *Figure 9.4*.

9.4.3 Real estate

In the real estate industry, data plays a vital role. We get following trades for this industry:

- **Market growth according to area**: As we know, area-wise data is constantly changing in the real estate industry. There is a need for this data to be analyzed as well as stored properly. Web scraping plays a very important role in the real estate industry, show in appropriate manner and design the site if required.

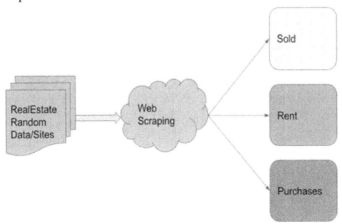

Figure 9.5: *Real estate data scraping*

- **Rental information**: Data is collected from different web-sites using web scrapers and stored into CSV/JSON format. Later we store this data into a database and represent it in a well-formatted website, which can be used for further comparison.

The following data is crucial in the real estate industry:

    ○ Price data

    ○ Address

    ○ Review

    ○ Property size

    ○ Trends

    ○ Rental price

    ○ City/State/zip Code

    ○ Images

In *figure 9.6*, you can see how this data might be saved in a CSV spreadsheet:

Figure 9.6: *Real Estate data in CSV format*

- **Appraisal in property value**: With the help of this data from web scraping, real estate agents are able to give recommendations to both sellers and buyers. This makes it easy for agents and the customers who approach them to get accurate information at a very fast rate.

On the basis of this data, it is easy to sell and predict the overall industry and give proper shape to it.

9.4.4 Finance sector

One of the most important sectors for web scraping is finance, where data collection is of tremendous importance. In this sector, huge amounts of data are collected and a specialized approach is needed for research and analysis. There are lots of sources in different forms from where data can be collected. Finance is a field where every small decision is crucial and these decisions can have major consequences down the line.

The stock market is also involved in the data scraping process and impacts both the investors and the functioning of the stock market.

As you can see in *figure 9.7*, we have a spreadsheet where data is collected from Yahoo Finance in the CSV format. This data is necessary for decision making and the accuracy of this data can have consequential outcomes:

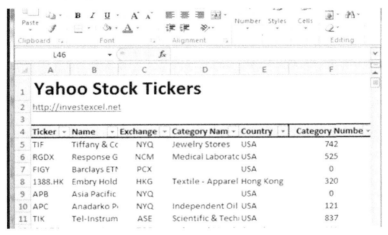

Figure 9.7: CSV format financial stock market data

It shows a list of different companies and their respective industries. We can also see the category numbers as well as the exchange the stock is listed on. This data has been crawled from using a Python crawler and stored into a CSV file.

Sometimes data is showing in the format where visuals are getting added and data is stored into databases.

Figure 9.8: Stock data

In *Figure 9.8*, we can see stock market data represented in a visual format. When data is presented effectively, it makes it easier to understand. We can credit all of this to web scrapers and crawlers to collect and organize this data using Python. With the help of web crawlers, we can collect useful data and present it in an easy to understand format.

9.5 Conclusion

In this chapter, we saw different aspects of web scrapers and tools. We also covered different industries where web scraping is used extensively. There are lots of use cases for web crawling like medical, all service based industry.

Points to remember

- Different use cases of industry

Questions

1. Does upper case matter in HTTP headers?

2. Which database type is getting used for storing crawled data?

3. Which format is the most suitable for representing scraped data?

Answers

1. Yes, it is case sensitive.

2. NoSQL database such as MongoDB.

3. JSON/CSV

Key terms

- **Use case list with web scraping as**: Market, medical, real estate, finance, etc.

CHAPTER 10
Industrial Benefits of Web Scraping

10.1 Introduction

In the last chapter we covered different use cases of web scraping. It is clear that web scraping plays a vital role in our day to day lives as well as its importance in planning and forecasting. In this chapter, we will go through the various benefits of web scraping and its role in different industries. We will cover how industries approach data collection and how this data is relevant for making future decisions. We will also introduce different fields and their key aspects.

10.2 Structure

As we learned in the last chapter, there are different use cases for web scraping in different industries; in this chapter we will shed more light on the industrial benefits of web scraping:

- Different industrial benefits of web scraping
- Examples of web scraping in e-commerce, marketing and sales, journalism, finance
- Importance of web scraping using Python libraries

10.3 Objective

Web scraping is a fast-growing practice that helps businesses collect data and structure this data in different formats such as JSON/CSV. This data can be represented visually as well which makes it easy to understand and use as per your needs.

- Benefits of web scraping in different industries.
- Different formats and formatted data for web scraping for fields like JSON/CSV
- Usability and clarity of data in different businesses due to web scraping

10.4 Benefits of web scraping

Scraping turns unstructured data into structured data and analyzes it and stores it into a central database for further use. Web scraping transforms the world in different application availability steps where it can be useful for industries as well better growth in all fields, these include:

- E-commerce
- Marketing and sales
- Journalism
- Finance

In *figure 10.1*, we can see that web scraping automation is the backbone for data collection and plays an important role to drive the real world with real use cases:

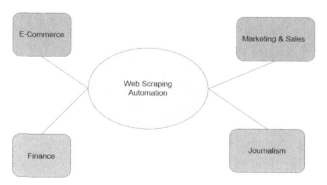

Figure 10.1: *Industries in which web scraping is involved*

As we can see, all the fields are more cores in the industries and act as a support system for other industries. Whenever anything new is introduced, it is important to monitor its data and usage. It is necessary to keep in mind that data is everywhere.

In web scraping following angles are also involved:

- **Real time data**: This is data which is collected or analyzed immediately as soon as it's available. Financial institutes are a prime example where real time data and analysis is required. It involves data stolen and any kind of fraud happens. Collecting real time data requires speed, effort, and other resources to ensure it is accurate.

- **Predictive analysis**: In this process, existing data is analyzed and processed to identify different patterns. On the basis of this data, businesses are able to make accurate predictions and decision.

- **Training models in machine learning**: In machine learning, huge amounts of data are required to train machine learning models. To ensure a high success rate, this data should be exact and accurate. On the basis of that data outputs, some models are trained and patterns get decided for future use.

10.4.1 Marketing and sales

Data plays a vital role in marketing and sales. Unless you have proper and competitor's data, nobody can succeed in the field of marketing. Web scraping allows business to collect important data for marketing in the following ways:

- What data have you collected?
- How much time do you require to collect the data?
- How do you plan to structure the data?
- In how many ways can you use that data?

On the basis of the above questions, the following data is essential for marketing and sales:

- Product name
- URL
- Description
- Price

- Brand name
- Brand information
- Rating
- Competitor's product list

If needed, product history could also include:

- **Leads**: It is very important to get proper leads in marketing. With the help of data, businesses can both generate leads and compare product pricing, information, and more.

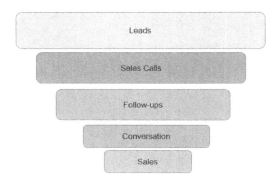

Figure 10.2: *Graph of marketing*

- **Sales call**: On the basis of lead data, marketing people call to the appropriate party and generate starting order before the exact order.

- **Follow-ups**: Continuous follow ups needed to get proper order in time, on the basis of that sales team do follow ups with the clients.

- **Conversation**: In this prosper conversation happens and order goes to the final step.

- **Sales**: This is the final step where order gets placed. A sale completes.

10.4.2. Journalism

This is one of the largest data collecting sectors where data is very important, and I have patience to make it a proper story from data.

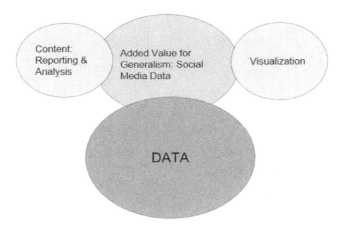

Figure 10.3: *Journalism data*

A variety of graphs and predictions are made by journalists using crawled data as a majority of people find it easier to understand a message when represented visually. In journalism, reporters have to create their own database from crawled data. They would have also own stories out of that, and that structural data makes it easy to represent in the real world without any error.

So, data gets more and important aspect as:

- Visualizing structured data can help capture a wider audience, more effectively.

- It allows journalists to create more effective stories and make it available to their audience.

- Research and analysis of stories from available structured data.

In journalism, three sectors come into picture:

- **Journalism investigates the topic**: It has itself a huge amount of data with scattered manners, so need to organize the same.

- **Reporters**: Reporters get structured data to show in front of different audiences.

- **Field of journalism**: In this field wrong information plays a very wrong impression and effect for a long term.

Hence, web scraping plays an important role in automation without any mistake data gets available in the structured format. Workflow the data information in the field of journalism:

- Get source information online from different websites.

- Defining logical pointers to collect useful data.

- Representing this data in a visual format, this may include animations, graphs, and more. It could be a different pattern to compare and showcase to the audiences.

- Show the visuals with correct wiring of different stories that should have logical statements and wirings between all showcases.

- Continuous monitoring is also important in this field to ensure accuracy, relevancy, and quality of data.

10.4.3 E-commerce

In e-commerce, collecting and analyzing data is important before you can commence your business. The success and growth of your business is dependent on targeted advertising as it allows your business to reach an audience that might be interested in your product or service. When anything gets crawled it is the basis of the surfing and need of the user, so automatically the business of e-commerce increases:

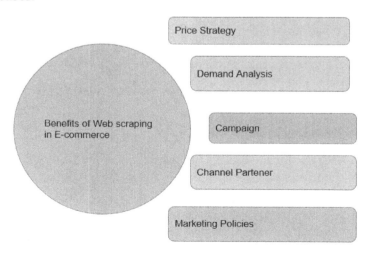

Figure 10.4: *E-commerce data*

Here you can see different strategies for reaching a wider audience in the e-commerce market. Through web scraping, businesses are able to analyze the demand, create targeted promotions, reach different channel partners, and engineer effective marketing policies. To achieve all of this, data crawling is essential to make your business a success.

The following data is essential for e-commerce marketing:

- Brand
- Section-wise distribution such as health, grocery, etc.
- Order history
- Price distribution
- Area-wise availability

Considering the above, we can determine the market demand and create customer profiles from collected data.

10.4.4 Finance

In finance, there are different sectors and instruments in which people can trade and invest. Historical data is very important for benchmarking and forecasting. With the help of web scraping, important data is collected and structured to understand trends over time:

	Date	Open	High	Low	Close	Volume
1	Date	Open	High	Low	Close	Volume
2	1June2020	701	725	710		
3	2June2020	708	735	702		
4	3June2020	704	720	706		
5	4June2020	709	732	708		
6	5June2020	712	741	704		
7	6June2020	703	734	704		
8	7June2020	706	751	712		

Figure 10.5: Data for Finance sector

As we can see in *figure 10.5,* all data sectors, how important web scraping is we came to know. It is very important to have structured data in all industries. Web scraping is used in finance for business development and research as well.

Following are the benefits of web scraping in the financial sector:

- **Financial data rating**: Availability of real-time data can be leveraged to make sound decisions and planning strategies.

- **Equity research**: Data is essential for equity research, analyzing company financials, performing ratio analysis, and more.

- **Wealth management**: It is useful to create wealth management for the future for individuals.

- **Market predictions**: Both current and historical data is used for predicting and creating sound market strategies. It enables organizations to identify valuable investments and reduce risk.

So in the preceding diagram you can see the different date wise data available with day high-low cost of share and the average also. So anyone can use that data to and invest in the share market with the risk. So gradually the risk of the investors decreased and profitability of the end user increased.

10.5 Importance of Python libraries in web scraping

Web scraping is made easier with Python libraries. In *figure 10.6,* we can see the combination of Python and web scraping in the past chapters. So, we know how Python automation plays an important role in web scraping.

Everything in the data world revolves around automation and Python has a powerful role in it. As industries grow, the demand for not only data but also well-formatted data increases. This cycle continues in all industries.

The power of Python in the industries automatically increases day by day which has big enhancement to the current situation. So all industries get benefits from web scraping in the growth of their own business. So at the end finance sector gets more import by collecting all other industries data with comparison:

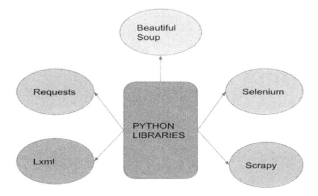

Figure 10.6: *Libraries of Python*

So, these libraries also have too much importance in automation.

10.6 Conclusion

In this chapter, we have seen the importance of web scraping in different industries. Overall, we have learned several benefits of web scraping in different types of businesses. As day by day all industries' markets are growing with the help of data. So in future also more data and their formatted structure will be needed as well.

Points to remember

In this chapter we have learned various web scraping benefits and the importance of Python libraries in web scraping automation:

- Different benefits of web scraping in industries.
- Importance of Python libraries

Questions

1. How do you avoid captcha requirements?
2. Which browser type is mostly getting used for crawling?

Answers

1. Using proxies.

2. Headerless browsers.

Key terms

- Different sectors of industry where web scraping is getting used like finance, journalism, e-commerce, etc.

Index

Printed in Great Britain
by Amazon

86214816R00078